AMERICAN DECORATION
A SENSE OF PLACE

AMERICAN DECORATION
A SENSE OF PLACE

THOMAS JAYNE

THE MONACELLI PRESS

Published in the United States by The Monacelli Press LLC

Library of Congress Control Number 2012940140

ISBN 978-158093-337-7

10 9 8 7 6 5 4 3 2 1

First edition

Design: Susan Evans, Design per se, New York

Printed in China

www.monacellipress.com

Acknowledgments

As I write this, we are mourning our friend and mentor, the legendary decorator Albert Hadley. He taught all of us who knew and worked with him ways to create extraordinary design. At heart of his process was gratitude. He frequently reminded me that interior decoration is a complicated process and that countless talented individuals contribute to the design of any refined interior.

Not only do I owe Albert countless thanks for encouraging my career—his influence is seen in many of the rooms in this book—but there are important debts as well to the remarkable patrons, tastemakers, architects, designers, craftsmen, and myriad others with whom I collaborate. I offer each of them my gratitude.

Nancy Romeu, who is creative director at Jayne Design Studio, is pivotal to my decorating. She is generous with her brilliant eye and assures that our design processes run well. Most important, she is my standard for decorum and charm. I am also grateful to my other colleagues at the studio, especially decorators Egan Seward and Erik Smith for their long association here. I have the greatest admiration for their commitment to innovation, beauty, and taste.

I value a circle of artists, historians, designers, and editors who aid my work more than I think they know, including Nadine and Simon Blake, Stephen Calloway and Susan Owens, Howard Christian, Robert Clepper, Elaine Greenstein, Eric Kahn, Jean Doris Kahn, David Kleinberg, Tim Knox and Todd Longstaff-Gowan, Maggie Lidy, Sarah Medford, Mitchell Owens, Melinda Papp, Peter Patout, Peter Pennoyer, Tom Savage, Deb Shriver, and Pilar Viladas. They have shown me design in new ways.

I am a decorator who sometimes finds myself an author. Fortunately, I do this with the influence of friends who write. Jeanne Sloane has guided my prose from my Winterthur Fellowship application to the present conjuring of this text; William Irvine, one of the most erudite men I know, read this text and informed every step with sage advice. Jane Lear's editorial eye, ironic and without malice, informs me every day. Jean O'Brien, who showed me the ideal of a perfect essay, reminds me good prose is organized much like good decoration.

Without my editor at The Monacelli Press, Elizabeth White, and her consummate professional acumen, this book would not exist. Thank you for giving me a home.

I am also grateful to the photographers represented here, especially Kerri McCaffety and Pieter Estersohn. The handsome presentation is the work of designer Susan Evans of Design per se.

It is my good fortune to be surrounded by a family, both natural and surrogate, especially Roger Jayne, Catharine Hedger, Diane Horn, Jane Adams and Scott Galupo, Abigail Galupo, Sam Galupo, Tim and Melissa Adams, my godchildren Grace Adams and Caroline Adams, Susan Jayne, Jayne McCoy, Betts Rockwell, Julia Burke, Julia Reed, and The Rev. Stephen Gerth.

One person above all who has furthered my career and this book is my partner, Richmond Ellis. I cannot convey the depths of his confidence and commitment in me over the past quarter century. This book is dedicated to him.

Contents

Library, Beekman Place, New York

AMERICAN DECORATION
A Sense of Place

My interest in American architecture and decoration, and ultimately my career as a decorator, began with my family's legacy of houses. Over a gradual migration across the country spanning nearly four hundred years, we kept track of many of places—crowded and medieval dwellings at Plymouth, eighteenth-century Long Island farmhouses with small rooms and low ceilings, a tavern in Vermont, my great-grandfather's Italianate villa with its handsome double parlors in Monticello, Iowa, and an aunt's surprising decision to forsake family furniture and "go Scandinavian Modern" in her ranch house in Texas. My grandfather was a civil engineer in Santa Barbara, and childhood visits to his Craftsman-style bungalow set in a fantastic subtropical garden and artistically furnished with antiques and mission furniture impressed me the most.

Eventually I learned how each of these houses, their interiors, and the people who lived in them, fit into the history of American design. My family also appreciated other people's old houses, and no vacation itinerary lacked places of historic merit. This longstanding interest has given me an understanding of what American decoration is and, I think, enhanced my ability to make attractive, comfortable, site-specific, and meaningful rooms.

Central to my understanding of this history is the rhetorical question "What is American decoration?" Considering the breadth of our continent, its myriad natural environments, and its role as a home to every ethnicity from hundreds of countries, I often reply, "Everything can be American," and I find it telling that there are no definitive elements forming a specific American style. Nevertheless, there are essential characteristics that in various combinations typify American rooms.

One important quality that fascinates me is that American houses reflect the place where they are built. Every quadrant of America has regional architecture that suits the natural environment and the culture of the people who live there. Houses in Maine often have sturdy exteriors that are relatively free of ornament to withstand the weather. Houses in the South often have high ceilings and multiple porches. Southwestern houses usually have thick walls—the earliest were of adobe—and courtyards to protect the rooms from abundant heat and light. I have come to understand that the ideal American room refers to its location, the region's vernacular architecture, comfort, and personal associations.

One of the most remarkable aspects of American design is that the diversity of our population encourages the use of virtually every style from traditional to modern, western to Asian, formal to informal. Asian art has always influenced American taste, and today it has increasing importance. However, historically America has largely looked to Europe for design inspiration, especially to France and England. Significantly, these quotations have not been verbatim. I think this is because of the diverse cultural background of Americans, as well as the fact that, until very recently, the scale of the houses was more modest.

At the University of Oregon, where I studied architecture and art history, and later in the decorative arts program at Winterthur, it was deemed imperative that we fully understand historic design in both England and France. I was fortunate to study in those countries with the Attingham Summer School as well as the Victorian and Furniture History Societies—all programs for in-depth examination of important houses guided by curators and scholars. It was on these visits that I understood, beyond textbook pages, the importance of aristocratic patronage for scale and quality, a tradition that necessarily does not exist in America.

I will never forget arriving at Attingham Park, my first visit to an English country house on a grand scale. It was the Fourth of July and the American flag was flying in our honor. We were received in the main hall, not the grandest of English examples, but still larger than almost any American entrance room. I remember walls of the most beautiful old pale green paint and a lovely informal arrangement of pink roses with grasses on a gilt-wood center table that connected the room to the landscape park. In the adjoining public rooms there was also an impressive level of refinement, especially the exemplary picture gallery with one of the first glass ceilings. This relatively minor English house is superior to every American house of the period. It affirmed for me that the scale of American rooms and the range of their contents are vastly different from their European counterparts.

Decorators and American Taste

During this time, I also examined the primary role of decorators in the history of American design. At the turn of the twentieth century, professional decorators became disseminators of style. Before the end of the previous century, European influence came through craftsmen, merchants selling domestic and imported luxury goods, and foreign publications illustrating changes in taste.

Elsie de Wolfe is considered the first American decorator. By her professional practice and her book, *The House in Good Taste* (1913), she influenced an entire generation of interior designers including, for example, Eleanor Brown, Ruby Ross Wood (de Wolfe's ghost writer), Billy Baldwin, Sister Parish, and my friend and mentor Albert Hadley. Each of these designers interpreted French and English taste for the American house.

For me the epitome of the adaptation of European design for America is the work of Parish-Hadley, the

firm where I started my career. Albert Hadley helped me understand that my training in American architecture and art history would be a natural fit in the world of interior design and encouraged me to open my firm. I think what distinguishes both Sister Parish and Albert Hadley from their counterparts is that they appreciated rather than discounted American decoration. In fact, many of their rooms intersperse classic American furniture and decorations with French and English pieces.

With this mix of decorative arts, Parish-Hadley helped develop and establish the core qualities of the best twentieth-century interiors. These include the creation of the best architecture as the foundation for good interior design—it is always easier to decorate a room with good scale and details, they often explained—the organization of rooms around a focal point, usually a work of art, and emphasis on including elements of comfort such as easy chairs, convivially placed, and convenient surfaces for drinks and books. These elements were all artfully modulated to give their rooms a timeless and settled character.

It is significant that just as there is no absolute definition of American decoration, within the Parish-Hadley tradition, there are no iconic elements such as a chair or table model that define their work. Of course there are iconic rooms, and some of my favorites—Mrs. Astor's library, Nancy Pyne's living room in New Jersey, and the sitting room in Albert's apartment—immediately come to mind.

The Influence of Winterthur and H. F. du Pont

Another great influence on my decoration is Henry Francis du Pont and the Winterthur Museum, to my eye the ultimate house museum created by one of America's most gifted decorators. As a graduate fellow, I spent two years studying 175 antique rooms filled with more than 60,000 objects used or made in

America from the seventeenth through the nineteenth centuries. At the time of the museum was created, there was a bias toward European design. Winterthur was created as a proof that an American room is often comparable in beauty, if not scale and enrichment, to its foreign counterpart.

Mr. du Pont was a gentleman and designed only his own projects. However, he had the eye for color, scale, and arrangement of a professional decorator and the insights of an historian that give his rooms a visual harmony as well as intellectual content. Once he described the perfect Winterthur curator as part librarian and part decorator, and I fully understand what he meant by this ideal. I find it telling that Jacqueline Kennedy asked Henry du Pont to chair the fine arts committee for the redecoration of the White House. She wanted to use a French decorator, but politics demanded that she rely on American advice. Sister Parish became the official White House decorator, while Stéphane Boudin, from Paris, quietly did the important design work. To mitigate the role of Boudin and champion American design, Mr. du Pont made a point of inviting Mrs. Kennedy to Winterthur to affirm that historic American houses could, to use his words, "be swell."

Several years ago Tom Savage, director of Museum Affairs at Winterthur, asked me to speak about Mr. du Pont's influences on my work. I was surprised, as I had never consciously imitated Winterthur or really thought about how it influenced me. Clearly I owe an important debt to his genius. The great neoclassical drawing room at Drumlin Hall, which we recently decorated with early nineteenth-century American furniture, shows his direct influence. It can also be seen in rooms I have decorated without Americana, such as the series of rooms for a collector of postwar art where the textiles are subtlety paired for rich harmonies to avoid high contrast with the works of art.

My Design Process

When I was 13, after reading Jacqueline Kennedy's guide to the White House, I painted my bedroom to match the Red Room. I installed my great-grandparents' Lincolnesque rococo revival bed and other family furniture of a similar ilk. This was especially radical as my family lived in a postwar house in Pacific Palisades, California. About this time our neighbor, artist Jean Kahn, suggested that I had a designer's eye and that I would become a decorator rather than a lawyer as I had planned. This idea horrified me, as the stereotype of an interior decorator was a far cry from my self-image as a future Supreme Court justice.

However, looking back to the first interior I designed, I see the nascent qualities that have become central to my work: creating American decoration from a wide combination of elements, both old and new, that are expressive of the occupant's place and personality.

My academic training stressed the importance of thorough research at the beginning of a project, and I have found that a successful room begins with taking stock of the history of the place, the people who lived there, and the region's historic design traditions. Equally important is a solid understanding of the needs and personality of the people who will use these rooms. To some, my interest in history might imply the creation of static "period" rooms more suited to historical reenactments rather than today's living. In fact, I only use historic research to inspire new design. As one critic put it, my work is grounded in historic antecedents but seen with my own uniquely modern lens.

I admire the sculptural qualities of antiques, their novel shapes and surfaces, which are unmatched by new pieces—an old table with handsomely turned legs, made of beautiful old-growth wood and a unique surface that comes with age, or a looking glass with its watery reflection and patinated gilt wood. I like to point out that except for rare exceptions where everything is designed at once—for example, the interiors by Frank Lloyd Wright—few of us live in rooms where everything is brand new. Instead the rooms are filled with pieces that represent generations. I pay attention to old objects, in part for their narrative history—where they are from, who owned them as relics or heirlooms—and also for inspiration for making new things. How the shapes of furnishings in a room relate to one another is paramount, especially since we tend to actively mix styles and periods. Very few pieces in my rooms match. Instead they relate visually in abstract ways.

The Importance of Color

Color is a principal asset in my work; many times we literally recolor the past by giving an antique piece a new hue. I think color can change almost anything. Color has been appreciated in different ways over time, and in fact new shades are constantly invented. Until modem times, creating a brightly colored object was often expensive, and the greater man-made world was largely in neutral tones. Bright colors stood out in a way they do not today. Now the world is brightly hued, and to compensate for this glare, many choose the refuge of white and beige environments. I try to find a balance with the color in my rooms, avoiding both colorless spaces and also those with wildly contrasting colors.

I am very aware that the perception of color changes, depending on the setting. This has to do with light and atmosphere, and the physics of how the human eye perceives color. This is why bright colors, often called tropical colors, look good in the lower latitudes and cannot be universally applied in other places. I remember an account of Mrs. Parish returning from London with a selection of chintzes, each of them attractive in English light. In the brighter atmosphere of New York, some of their colors just "did not work." I have similar experiences preparing decorating schemes in New York. Even mentally compensating for the difference in the light of another location, such as Maine or Florida, I have had schemes wash out or not match when we reappraise them on site.

Quality

It is an understatement to say that quality is essential to good decoration. Of course one can make a seemingly attractive room with inexpensive goods. But in time, often a very short time, it will fail. I recall a *New Yorker* cartoon that showed a man pontificating with the caption "I don't want much, but I want it to be good quality." I agree to the point that it is best to start a home with good things and add to it, rather than fill a house with compromised choices that will have a short useful life. Finding quality is often not about price, but about appropriate choices.

An ideal room makes an immediate good impression and there are further refinements that only become apparent over time—whether it is a reference to some historic building detail, the nuance of a grouping of furniture, or the details of the curtains. Often this comes from custom elements. I think it is difficult to make a memorable room without at least something bespoke to tie the room together, even if it is just a special paint color or a simple pair of curtains.

Many of the furnishings in our rooms are artisanal, individually made by various craftsmen. A large portion of the upholstery is handmade with natural materials, including solid wood frames, hand-tied springs, and curled horsehair—furniture that will endure a lifetime. The important fabrics we use are often specially designed and handcrafted in both traditional and modern techniques. Damasks are sometimes woven on antique looms using historic documents as patterns, and we have printed goods using computers and digital technology. We also use custom passementerie, which in my opinion, even the most contemporary interiors can require. We work with talented cabinetmakers who work to the highest historic standards. Several shops make metalwork to our designs, while other artists create *églomisé* panels and hand-blocked wallpaper.

Clearly I am not afraid to use classic elements such as established upholstery models and pedestal dining tables. As Albert Hadley pointed out, there is a reason why they work. Still it is important to be careful not to use them as a crutch, or to overuse them. I remember reading *The Decoration of Houses*, Edith Wharton's seminal book on decoration written with Ogden Codman. Wharton and Codman state, "A classic is a classic not because it conforms to certain structural rules, or fits certain definitions; it is a classic because of a certain eternal and impressive freshness."

In the end, I always remember that no amount of research or historic perspective can lead directly to beautiful design. The past provides reference points that can serve as springboards to new and appealing interiors. Certainly just because something is old does not necessarily mean it is attractive. As my partner, Richmond Ellis, regularly affirms, "If it wasn't pretty then, it's probably not pretty now." Yet, along with artistic merit, I have come to understand that the ideal American room refers to its location, the region's vernacular architecture, comfort, and personal associations.

I believe that each of us has unique gifts. I think mine include the eye of a designer and the philosophical approach of a historian. These gifts have been manifested beginning with my youthful take on the White House Red Room to the decoration of wonderful houses in New England, the South, and the West—a lifetime and career of considering American decoration and its sense of place.

House with the Golden Stair

New York, New York

THERE IS SOMETHING ROMANTIC about having a house in the city—in this case one set in the middle of a world capital. You are at the center of a metropolis, but you can also escape from the urban bustle into your own self-contained world.

Brownstones, an American variant of a townhouse, proliferated in East Coast cities in the late nineteenth century. While their facades may be repetitive and their original plans formulaic (party walls with a stair running alongside, a floor with two proper parlors, and floors of bedrooms above), these houses offer a relatively broad range of architectural detail, and time has allowed for inventive change. Their interiors now extend from those in perfect original condition, with Victorian woodwork, marble, tile, and elaborate fittings—I know of one that still has fittings for gas lights—to loft-like spaces. Many, like this one designed by A. B. Ogden in 1889, were divided into rental apartments.

Architect Basil Walter was commissioned to return the building to single-family use. His plan focused on centering the staircase and adding two large skylights overhead. There was concern about safety in a multi-floor stairwell so together we designed a modern staircase influenced by a series of nineteenth-century models, including the architecture of Sir John Soane, Parisian elevators, and the yellow glass windows found in English and American houses to create the effect of sunlight, even on the dimmest days. We also used gold mesh, so-called chicken wire, from the French decorative arts tradition.

Within the new floor plan, an effort was made to keep as many of the original architectural details as possible. About 30 percent survived, to which we added other nineteenth-century details, including panels of architectural mirror to reflect the available light—also an oblique homage to Soane. To blend the old woodwork with the new, almost everything was painted to resemble the wood grain of medium-brown walnut.

The first floor is an old-fashioned, multi-purpose living hall, acting as foyer, sitting room, and stair landing. A wide passage, buffered with curtains, opens to a more formal back parlor that is reserved for family quiet time.

At the rear of the first floor is a formal but comfortable parlor with walls painted in an unexpected shade of chartreuse found in the antique Sultanabad. This carpet was made in the late nineteenth century, about the same time the house was built.

This floor features a collection of English and Continental furniture that our clients assembled when they lived in London. These furnishings are grander than the house itself, and we took great care, by arrangement and decoration, to allow them to fit comfortably into the newly designed spaces. In particular, we mirrored the chimneybreast to display an eighteenth-century Irish mirror and English gilt-wood sconces.

Notable rooms upstairs are the library and the daughters' room. Located in what is a rare townhouse penthouse, no longer allowed by zoning, the library is often flooded with the sun from skylights over the stair and the desk. In a nod to Victorian precedents, we incorporated pieces of colored glass in the skylight design. The walls are paneled in leather to enforce a bookish appearance.

The daughters share a floor with a playroom, workroom, small terrace, and a large bedroom. To create privacy, we made their beds tent-like, customizing metal frames with their monograms and crowning each one with a different bouquet of feathers and butterflies. The beds sit against mirrored walls concealing cabinet doors, each with individual compartments for the girls to store their treasures.

The walls of the living hall are covered in plain weave fabric embossed with a damask pattern, a variation of a richer material that might have hung in this room when it was new. The sofa, covered in suede and tapestry and finished in bullion fringe, is adapted from a model associated with the influential Italian decorator Renzo Mongiardino. Bo Bartlett's portrait of his daughter, hanging above, seems especially suitable for a household of three girls.

While the seven-story stairwell is enclosed for safety, the sides are transparent so every floor benefits from the large skylight that caps the space. Turned metal, mahogany, colored glass, chicken wire, and decorative paint were all used in its composition.

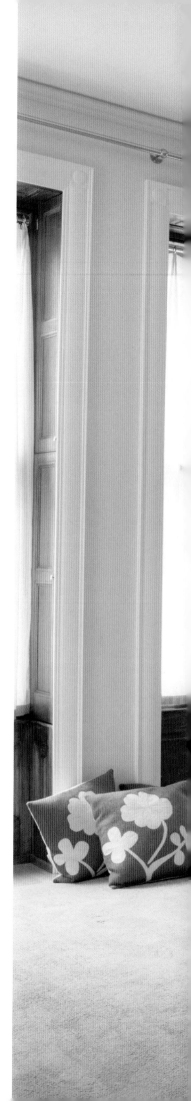

The skylight in the study has a collar of mirror and colored glass. The new oak woodwork, chosen for its association with historic libraries, is clear-finished with inlaid leather panels.

In the daughters' room, the original window surrounds were preserved. They contrast with the new wall of mirrored panels that are also cabinet doors. The room-sized cotton carpet, once a staple of New York interiors, is soft, durable, and somewhat old-fashioned.

Youthful Historicism

New York, New York

I REMEMBER ONCE SPEAKING to Mark Hampton, one of America's most important traditional decorators, about midcentury modern decoration, a term that was not yet coined. He had firsthand experience, having apprenticed with David Hicks, the British decorator, who perfected a style of modern interior design with inventive furnishings and geometric carpets in Pop colors. Mark felt that modern taste was doomed to go out of style, and that so-called traditional decoration would always endure because of its timeless appearance. I remember thinking, in my callow youth, that traditional style is by its nature out-of-date—and perhaps that is why it endures.

I now understand that a tradition must exist or it is dead; therefore, a recently decorated traditional room is as contemporary as a house full of the newest styles. I also believe that no matter the furniture, it is possible to date a room by design elements such as color, pattern, and even functional, mundane elements, such as lampshades. Regardless of the historic accuracy of a house and its details, the taste of the creators always surfaces over time. And, whatever the style—old or new—the best examples always look good and have the longest staying power. The rooms in this townhouse, decorated some fifteen years ago, are arguably timeless.

The house, built in the 1870s as a brownstone, was remodeled in 1917 in the Federal Revival taste by Murphy & Dana as part of a sweeping trend transforming Upper East Side brownstones. The interiors had been remodelled at the time, and the rooms on each end were opened to the full width of the building. Because the house sits on a particularly wide lot, this makes a wonderful difference.

For the decoration we aimed for what I call a "youthful historicism" that was relatively simple, but of the best quality. As inspiration, I consciously and subconsciously referenced early-twentieth-century Anglo-American design books, taking inspiration from two of my favorites: Emily Post's *The Personality of a House* and *A Monograph of the Work of Mellor, Meigs & Howe*. We created rooms with a relatively spare arrangement of works of art and furniture, usually of a sculptural nature, breaking with the elaborate so-called country house taste in America that was popular in the 1980s.

Occasional furniture plays an important role in all comfortable decoration today. This room has a pair of vintage mirrored tables that I found in Palm Beach, a circular round table adapted for us by John Boone from an historic design by Paul Jones, and an Egyptian Revival Thebes stool by the window—all seemingly modest furniture without which the room would be incomplete.

In the second-floor living room, the autumnal hues of the nineteenth-century Japanese screen set the color scheme. The grand Indian carpet—the first item we selected together for the house—complements its tone perfectly. To begin the project, as I often do, we deliberated over several choices, and the decision to go ahead with this carpet was the foundation for the decor. The rest of the furniture in the room followed—an eclectic mix, including a pair of lacquer trunks, a desk at the window, and a Regency chair with a curving shape. For the curtains, in an Upper East Side townhouse where sunlight is always at a premium, we incorporated tall panels of yellow silk without pelmets— a dynamic way to further the sense of light in the space.

The dining room had a similar 1920s ethos. This was designed for our clients by Peter Pennoyer to showcase an eighteenth-century Chinese wallpaper of exemplary beauty that I had bought in London for the space. Anglo-Indian dining chairs, a Georgian table, an Aesthetic Movement sideboard by the English firm Talbot, and a candelabrum by Louis Comfort Tiffany formed a new mix with an old-fashioned air.

We built the master bedroom around a fantastic mantel that the client had also bought before the purchase of the house. I was asked as part of the interview process if I could incorporate it into the room. It could have been a case of what I call "stump the decorator," but by making it the focal point and using a chintz that has some of the same blues and other complementary colors, we were able to make a beautiful and memorable room.

A blue-and-white porcelain mantelpiece
from the turn-of-the-twentieth century
anchors the bedroom. A late-nineteenth-
century English needlepoint carpet
in front of the hearth helps to balance
the composition. The restored passementerie tassels for the Lalique glass
light fixture enhance the romantic
nature of the room.

High-Style Americana

New York, New York

THE BEST EARLY AMERICAN FURNITURE was extremely expensive and luxurious when it was made in eighteenth-century colonial cities. Still, whenever I mention that a house or apartment will be furnished with Americana, eyes glaze over with visions of homespun cloth, lamps made of butter churns, and spinning wheels. I think high-quality American decorative arts look their best in formal settings, and I endeavored to create that level of grandeur for this superlative collection.

The luxury of the rooms and the collection is announced in the front hall, which features enriched doorways, with mahogany doors capped by pediments. We supported this architecture with painted panels in damask patterns on the walls, intentionally making the color soft, but with enough contrast to read as a crisp design. On center with the front door is a mirror—or, to use the older term, "looking-glass"—of extraordinary quality. It dates from the mid-eighteenth century and is celebrated for its size and open fretwork.

This hall and its decoration lead easily into the living room, where the scheme is principally of green and yellow, integrated with some pink and blue, and devised to work with a remarkable early-nineteenth-century English carpet. It provides enough pattern for the entire room and supports the use of a single shade of green for almost all the furniture. Only the type of fabric varies: an ottoman weave is used on the new upholstered pieces and a silk damask in an eighteenth-century pattern for the antiques.

En suite fabric—the use of the same fabric in the same color—was a customary decorating device in the eighteenth century. We furthered this notion by using the damask for the curtains, which are designed with pelmets of swags and jabots in the eighteenth-century style to enhance the relatively simple architecture of the space. We also added the fireplace mantel in the Georgian style to enrich the details of the room. It is about the same date as this early-twentieth-century apartment building.

The wing chair and lolling chair in the living room are both rare examples of furniture made in Charleston, South Carolina, during the eighteenth century. The Chinese garden seats next to them are nineteenth century. Originally intended for outdoor use, these seats are now also used as small tables.

The adjoining library is paneled in mahogany that was french-polished to match the finish quality of the antiques. The color scheme is related closely to the painting by Jane Peterson that hangs on the central panel. The book-cases are filled with a well-used library dedicated to the American arts and examples of Chinese Export porcelain. Across the hall is the study. The room is arranged around an English breakfront that holds a collection of American silver, including pieces by the patriot silversmith Paul Revere.

By today's standards, the dining room is especially formal, with a set of fourteen chairs in a matching design associated with eighteenth-century New York. The room is enlivened by bright blue walls, a color found in many houses of the eighteenth century but not expected today. The salmon-pink curtains, made for the room by Claremont with tapes woven with green laurel leaves, are also specially colored to flatter the antique wood and the Persian carpet.

The Chinese lacquered low table was made for export. Interspersed with the books is a collection of Chinese Export ceramics and a group of eighteenth-century Meissen birds.

On the sideboard in the dining room is a notable nineteenth-century French mantel clock with a figure of George Washington, a hero of both the American and French Revolutions. Across the room is an eighteenth-century Philadelphia chest-on-chest with its original finial carved in the shape of a basket of flowers. The neoclassical girandole mirror between the windows is probably English, but it is a type that was imported to America in the eighteenth and nineteenth centuries.

An English secretary bookcase in the study now displays Colonial American silver. The upper cases of this form were designed to house books, a great luxury when this piece of furniture was made.

The bedroom displays a collection of eighteenth-century blue-and-white ceramics. The printed linen curtains have valances to control the morning light. Wall-to-wall carpet allows the furniture to sit comfortably in the room.

A Place of Their Own

New York, New York

OUR CLIENTS—TWO BROTHERS—inherited this apartment from their mother. Once they had used it as a pied à terre for a year, and suffered through the old French chairs collapsing, they decided it was time to interview decorators. I am always careful when readying a home for the next generation. It is an act of balancing sentiment and familiarity with the future. Often, it is a sinking burden to keep everything you inherit—even if it is from someone you love. I have always found it best to combine the functional with the sentimental and keep only a few objects for purely sentimental reasons.

Here, our first act was to deaccession the fragile chairs. And now, after a series of slight architectural changes and redecoration, they are not missed—especially with the addition of some of the clients' own furniture and the reinstallation of their remarkable collection of art. The apartment is located in an elegant riverfront building developed in 1930 by the Rockefellers, and designed by Sloan & Robertson, with Corbett, Harrison & MacMurray, the firm that was creating Rockefeller Center at the same time. Constructed just as the Depression descended on the city, the rooms were graciously planned to suit the discerning tenants but were not ostentatious. The architectural detailing is spare, reflecting the Art Deco movement and perhaps the economic climate as well.

This relative simplicity served as the perfect foil for the art collection, which spans the history of twentieth-century painting and is classically juxtaposed with pre-Columbian ceramics. While our decoration pays homage to this inheritance and the period of the building, we simplified our schemes for the rooms and then focused on key pictures and furniture. For example, in the living room, we added a bright red center table. A dynamic counterpoint to the quieter furniture in the room, it is also something of a spellbreaker, announcing that the apartment has new occupants. In the dining room we reinstalled a twentieth-century baroque console and supplied simplified dining chairs.

Throughout the apartment, the subtle but noteworthy play of pattern unifies the space, creating enough decorative support to complete the interiors without competing with the works of art. We achieved this by furnishing fabrics, carpet, and, in the principal rooms, Pierre Finkelstein's paintwork,

In the library, paintings by Pablo Picasso from his Blue and Cubist periods are hung together for contrast. The Aubusson carpet from the first part of the twentieth century is a family piece that provides the key decoration for the room. The bookcases have a collection of pre-Columbian works of art. The lamps are American.

whose textures are so fine they are imperceptible until closely examined. This infusion of color firmly establishes that this is a private home rather than an art gallery.

Hanging this collection of art was a special effort. It is not easy to install myriad paintings in random sizes and various styles. In a private house, a successful arrangement of paintings involves the use of color on the walls, part art history, and part intuitive taste for relationships in the compositions. Intuition often prevails, as most people respond more easily to visual effects than scholarly connections. A handsome hang, as we call it, is achieved by taking the time for trial and error to perfect arrangements, sometimes moving pictures to different rooms—and sometimes just by inches—to look their best. In this apartment, spectacular the views of the East River, the 59th Street Bridge, and beyond provide a dynamic balance to the art and decoration.

The family assembled here for the first time last Christmas, returning to an apartment that not only honors their mother's legacy but also provides a place for them and the future.

In the living room, paintings are paired with fine examples of decorative arts, including a rare red German center table by Otto Zapf from 1967 and a pair of Swedish urns designed by Ivar Johnsson for Nafveqvarns Bruk, now with blue glass tops, which serve as side tables.

A Louis XVI commode sits beneath a painting by Georges Braque in its original Parisian frame.

The console table and chandelier, installed
in the dining room in the 1960s, are in
the eighteenth-century French taste.
I appreciate their sculptural qualities,
which allow them to be successful
companions to twentieth-century
artworks, including paintings by
Max Ernst and Jackson Pollock. The
walls and the curtains closely match
in color and tone to focus attention on
the works of art and also to conceal the
irregular architectural beams typical
of early-twentieth-century high-rise
construction in New York.

Two bedrooms with river views are decorated en suite using a chintz with yellow and brown flowers and pale blue walls. The gunmetal bed, custom made for the room, is covered with a vintage Indian sari. The Persian Malayer village carpet from the early twentieth century has a related pattern. Sven Lukin's Construction, *1961, hangs in the smaller bedroom.*

A Designer's Legacy

New York, New York

I LIKE THE TERM "SUCCESSOR DECORATOR"—someone who builds upon what an earlier decorator established in the same place. He or she furthers a legacy of great decoration by refreshing, renewing, and developing rooms that are already well designed. Often the rooms I decorate have interesting histories that should be honored. I became fully aware of this when I was working for the Colony Club in New York. Designed by the architects Delano & Aldrich, the clubhouse had interiors rich with decorations supplied by Elsie de Wolfe, among others. I was certainly mindful of that legacy when I had the privilege of redecorating the club's ballroom and visitors' reception room. And, in fact, I was fortunate to meet these clients through my work there.

This apartment also had a rich inheritance. Within a few steps into the front hall, I knew a great designer had worked there before me. Donald Oenslager, the clients' uncle, first decorated the rooms in the early 1960s. A Tony Award–winning set designer famous for *Anything Goes*, *A Majority of One*, and *Major Barbara*, he guided the decor of this apartment's public rooms with rich color schemes and arrangements that brilliantly highlighted the family's eclectic collection of American paintings and antiques, as well as the remarkable hooked rugs made by the patriarch of the household, a device for quitting smoking while watching football.

In the front hall, Oenslager installed Chinese paper on an aluminum ground with a ceiling stippled in shades of orange. We did very little in this space, other than touching up the paint and arranging sculptures by Tom Otterness on a Chinese table. This hall is a preamble to the collections displayed throughout the apartment.

We did more in the library. The carpet, with its inventive design based on a Japanese moss garden, formed the basis for the new fabrics. Comfortable upholstered furniture was added to the existing collection of European and American decorative arts. In the dining room, we also restored the carpet, a design based on Chinese fabrics with bat motifs, covered the Chippendale chairs in embossed leather, and adjusted the green of the walls to feature the warm palette of the paintings and a large sculpture by Dale Chihuly.

A Stuart Davis painting of Greenwich
Village hangs over the fireplace in the
living room opposite a painting of ships
by Richard Bosman and a sculpture by
Roy Lichtenstein. Mirrored window
reveals expand the views and light, a
popular device in apartments overlooking
Central Park.

The dining room retains the applied
moldings typical of the 1920s when this
building was constructed; the ceiling,
covered in gold tea paper first installed
in the 1960s, was recently restored.
The dark green color with a warm cast
flatters the works of art, including the
painting by Anne Abrams hanging above
a New England sideboard from the first
half of the nineteenth century.

For the first few years we worked on this apartment, we made it a priority to conserve and repair the living room, especially the vintage Jack Lenor Larsen furnishings. Their rich beige and blue tones were classic, exactly what made him famous. Finally, when these fabrics wore out, we developed a new scheme, also in blue silk, and added as a counterpoint an Asiatic fabric in a tapestry weave. While it is more colorful than the Larsen fabrics, it plays well with contemporary art recently added to the collection. There is a new carpet of blue-green silk and the walls are covered in beige raffia.

Clearly the rooms look renewed and now very much of the twenty-first century. However, to the benefit all who use them, there is a strong presence of a certain favorite uncle with a remarkable eye.

We kept the furniture plan of the library open, in part because the room is used in so many ways, but mainly to display the carpet with its handsome design based on Japanese moss gardens. The collection of antiques includes an American wing chair, a Continental open armchair, and an English pedestal desk.

Decoration as Collage

Philadelphia, Pennsylvania

THIS TOWNHOUSE WAS built in the 1860s in an early neoclassical style and was remodeled by every subsequent generation. The 1900s saw the addition of classic paneled library and installation of reclaimed eighteenth-century Georgian mantels and windows reflecting the period's pervasive Colonial Revival taste. The 1930s brought an atrium of coral stone. When our clients bought the property, the house had been loosely divided into apartments and offices. As we began the project, we were confronted with a decision: should we restore the house to a single date—standard practice in some preservation projects—or selectively preserve what we thought was the most attractive and add to what was there? We chose the latter, making the conscious choice to augment and improve upon what we found. We wove all the parts together, making a larger opening between the front and back parlor with a so-called column screen, creating a rich but unifying color scheme, which included newly painted medium-blue floors, a new stone floor in the atrium, and the addition of fantastic entry-hall gates, commissioned by our clients from Albert Paley.

The rooms now fit more easily together and provide a setting for a collection of art and decorative arts that is as eclectic as the architectural setting. The core of the clients' wide-ranging furniture collection was assembled for a modern house. In that house, with its glass curtain walls and rectilinear geometries, their silhouettes had been juxtaposed with the sharp lines of the architecture. This historic house provided a more complicated background. I took great care to make sure that the furniture worked with the architecture and that the relationship between the two was simultaneously enriched and facile.

There are three approaches to using antiques in current decoration: create period rooms that reflect a certain date; furnish rooms with antiques from the same date, but not necessarily intended to all be in the same room; create a mix of old and new pieces selected for their shape, color, and patina. The contrast of the blue-lacquered Parsons dining table surrounded by the Portuguese chairs is a strong example of the third option. The end wall of the dining room is an early-nineteenth-century shopfront, which connects to the generous stone atrium. This is furnished with a collection of antique wicker.

An early-twentieth-century Spanish carpet has a relaxed symmetry that supports the variety and quality of the furniture in living room: a pair of Continental tables with bird-form bases, an English Chippendale sofa, and a large and finely executed English rococo mirror whose scale allows it to command almost an entire wall.

LEFT

The rich collection of architectural elements in the dining room is unified by wallpaper with an eighteenth-century English pattern of alternating stripes. Over the commode is one of a pair of gouaches by Franz Kaisermann. These capriccios, one depicting the Arch of Titus and the other the Temple of Sibyl at Tivoli, complement the architectonic theme of the room. The dining table from the 1970s is newly lacquered in blue.

RIGHT

We replaced a pair of low doors with a column screen between the living and dining rooms to take advantage of the ceiling height and to allow light into them from two sides. The far wall of the living room is an old shop front installed in the early twentieth century.

The bedrooms have an equally diverse mix of furniture. One has a chrome four-poster bed with a neoclassical girandole looking-glass with a beautiful antique surface. Another is covered in hand-blocked paper reproducing an early American pattern in bright colors, paired with a Maurice Sendak drawing of a character from *Where the Wild Things Are* and contemporary chairs with backs patterned like paper doilies. These rooms, like the others in the house are what I call "decoration as collage."

ABOVE

The relief over the fountain has an early Philadelphia history. It was carved by Giuseppe Jardella at the end of the eighteenth century for a folly on the Morris estate and later used on the facade of Benjamin Latrobe's Chestnut Street Theater.

OPPOSITE

When we started, we found the red Gothic chairs in the house. They now furnish the stair hall, along with a runner patterned after a nineteenth-century American example.

This bedroom has an early neoclassical mantel reinstalled here around 1900. The surround is composed of eighteenth-century Dutch tiles with magnesium decoration.

RIGHT

Our clients bought the chairs with doily-shaped backs on a trip to Milan; the Sendak drawing was purchased at a charity auction.

Enriched Decoration

New York, New York

AT THE FIRST DESIGN MEETING for a project, I like to "reach," as they say, and present my best thinking, no matter how grand it might be, with the understanding that these ideas will be adapted and tailored to our clients' responses. At the inaugural meeting for this project, I offered the concept that within this relatively small two-bedroom apartment, each room would have a distinct theme and personality, much like rooms found in grand historic houses.

I suggested that the living room feature boldly painted walls based on a pattern for an eighteenth-century English dress silk, the second bedroom be turned into a library in the Egyptian Revival taste, and the bedroom be hung with Chinese wallpaper with views of villages. The dining room would be draped to resemble a tent, and the two connecting halls would be covered in aubergine silk.

All of this, of course, ran counter to the accepted wisdom that in smaller spaces it is best to keep things neutral and free of large patterns. Suggesting a contrarian view is an approach I call "advanced decorating," or decorating that is, at least at first, not easy to appreciate or adopt. In this case, our client liked them all, and now she has a very personal and handsome apartment filled with delightful spaces.

The living room walls are covered in canvas painted by Anne Harris, based on 1707 designs for English dress silk by James Lehman. The pattern, dramatic but modulated so as not to overwhelm the room, is visually balanced by the weight of a Venetian fireplace and the frames of the paintings, especially a fanciful portrait reputedly of Marie Antoinette, and a series of abstract flowers, also by Anne Harris.

Two Egyptian-style bookcases with cavetto cornices and inlaid with the eyes of Horus, a symbol of protection, royal power, and good health, are the signature elements of the library, along with a collection of archaeological artifacts. The bedroom is also densely patterned with Chinese wallpaper commissioned for the room from Gracie. The furnishing fabrics are intentionally quiet to combine with the paper and give the room a calm nature.

LEFT AND RIGHT

The tented dining room has a Central European chandelier, remarkable collages by noted designer and artist James Mont, and a group of nineteenth-century English porcelain, including two vases decorated with polychrome flowers.

OVERLEAF

Even within the precepts of so-called traditional decorating, every actively used room should include contemporary elements. The low table in front of the fireplace and, arguably, the treatment of the walls reflect this concept.

The dining room is at the center of the apartment with the front hall, living room, and kitchen opening into it. It is tented in part to balance the four asymmetric doorways and to eliminate the awkwardness of multiple doors.

Now this apartment is enriched to the point where it looks much larger than it is, suggesting that painting everything neutral colors and eliminating pattern might, in fact, make places look smaller.

Many of the windows in this apartment
are arched and almost touch the ceiling.
In order to install shades and curtains, we
made window frames with deep reveals.
Each room displays portraits from the
collection our client has assembled over
her lifetime. Here an English portrait is
flanked by views of Egypt by David
Roberts.

The bedroom is hung with paper painted
with Chinese village scenes. The clean
lines of the dressing table bring the room
up to date. The carpet in the foreground is
a rare Bidjar Sampler.

Pied à Terre for the Past

Charleston, South Carolina

I WAS FIRST INTRODUCED to Charleston and to this client by Tom Savage, at the time curator and director of museums for the Historic Charleston Foundation. He sums the city up as "the Colonial city most connected to British taste." To this day, Charleston continues to have an Anglo-American legacy rich in eighteenth- and early-nineteenth-century buildings. They have survived in large part because of the city's reverses after the Civil War when, according to the famous aphorism, "people were too poor to paint and too proud to whitewash." When times improved, residents had the foresight to establish one of the first organizations to create a revolving fund to secure threatened buildings of historic merit.

This Federal townhouse from 1817, with its remarkable parlor floor, is now in fine condition because of Historic Charleston, but also in large part due to the efforts of Rob and Jane Hicklin. The ground floor, which has always been commercial, now houses Rob's business, the Charleston Renaissance Gallery; upstairs, "over of the store," is this lovely retreat and a place to display their private collections.

When approaching a decorating commission, there is always great value in learning everything possible about a project and its site—a notion I learned studying historic preservation. This preface to working with historic structures has served me well in every commission, elucidating what is important about a place and what to preserve, and also what can be effectively improved. Some designers might find this knowledge constraining, but I find it informative and, in fact, a source of creative inspiration.

At the same time that we were working on the Hicklins' house, Historic Charleston was restoring the Nathaniel Russell House, an important Federal building with beautiful interiors. Based on their paint research—the chemical examination of historic paints to reestablish original paint colors—and evidence found in the Hicklins' rooms, we used a palette of so-called stone colors, which were popular when these houses were built. Happily, these shades have the advantage of setting off the paintings well—strong enough to balance their rich colors—and appealing to contemporary taste. After discovering that one room had been wallpapered, we selected a period pattern used in America in the early nineteenth century.

I think paintings can look good against many wallpaper patterns, especially dense designs with colors with low contrasts, and this paper has the composition to work well with the paintings.

One of the special attributes of the house was the intact original woodwork. Working with architect John "Chip" Laurens, we had the woodwork restored—in fact, thoroughly cleaned by two very focused conservators with dental tools—so that it looked crisp and revived. The only missing element, the mantel in the living room, was replaced with a period example Rob found on King Street, Charleston's antiques row.

In preservation circles, there is often a dilemma whether to install curtains over enriched, often historic woodwork, especially since many historic designs cover the architecture with elaborate drapery. The Russell House research documents evidence of screw holes, for cloak pins, at the top of the windows, which informed our curtain design: a swag that hangs below the frame. I like them because they reflect historic evidence and also have modern appeal.

Decorating within a historically important context is always a balance between period verisimilitude and the personal comforts expected today. I often arrive at comfort, at the expense of authenticity, by employing fully upholstered chairs and sofas contrasted with select antiques. Here, I took the so-called "period room" approach and arranged the rooms with the Hicklins' superb collection of American antiques and works of art, which are all contemporaneous with the house. Arguably there is not a comfortable place to sit, and in a full-time residence, this antiquarian approach would be unusual. However, in this pied à terre, the decoration does not have to be practical, and the imagination of the past takes precedence.

ABOVE

In contrast to the public rooms, the bedroom is simply furnished with an antique bedstead.

OPPOSITE

A magnificent linen press made in Charleston in the early nineteenth century dominates the study. The valance, with swags and cloak pins, is patterned after historic documentation found in Charleston.

The carved wood architectural detail in the living room is typical of Low Country houses. The armchairs with their scrolling arms are rare American examples based on French models. The upholstery was chosen based on period evidence with sharp and crisp silhouettes in the neoclassical taste.

Ancient Allée

Green Pond, South Carolina

THERE IS AN ALMOST HEART-STOPPING sense of arrival for White Hall Plantation, with its atmospheric allée of ancient live oak trees draped with Spanish moss. Combined with that other leitmotif of American antebellum plantations, the white-columned portico, this house has a substantial presence that demands to be reflected inside.

In fact, the house was not a grand neoclassical pile reminiscent of *Gone With the Wind*, but instead a relatively simple house from the early twentieth century. It is plain enough that another owner might have torn it down in favor of a more expansive place. Nevertheless, the house has the authenticity of age, and it is one of the region's beloved country seats. I proposed that it could be agreeably improved with the restrained decoration typical of Low Country plantations, a style that favors early American and English furniture, Persian carpets—often with red and blue grounds—relaxed upholstery, old-fashioned wallpaper, and sporting art. This traditional decorative approach is handsome and somewhat modest, and it would allow us to create interiors worthy of the plantation's character.

Pivotal to our design was improving the central hall, the obvious hyphen to the allée of oaks. Here we made the only architectural changes, adding two classical arches between the foyer and the stair and another into the living room. Not only did this enrich the entrance sequence to bring it up to the level of the columned facade, but the arches also suggested additional height in a low space. The stair was redesigned after local Georgian examples, and the modern strip-oak floors were replaced with wide boards of old Southern pine. We wrapped the room in wallpaper painted for the space with a traditional pattern of branches and flowers supplemented with local plants, including the state tree of South Carolina, the palmetto, and magnolia grandiflora. Now after the dramatic approach through the live oaks, the hall continues this procession and gives an appropriate sense of arrival.

We carried the color scheme of the wallpaper into the living room, incorporating green curtains specially embroidered in yellow and red to enhance the modestly scaled 1920s windows. Off this room is a well-loved sitting room with a mural from the mid-twentieth century that is

important to the house's history. We found printed floral linen—also evocative of Low Country style—whose scale and colors perfectly suited the mural and the space.

Meanwhile, in some rooms, we made the judgment to do nothing since their "as found" condition was perfect. A notable example was the gun room. Originally arranged, I suppose, in the 1920s with a checkerboard floor and a carefully designed system of shelves and hooks now charmingly aged, we decided to leave it well alone.

Because of the social nature of this house, the dining room is one of the most important spaces. The architecture was also quite plain so we decided to contrast its simplicity against a damask wallpaper. Its pattern, which has been in continuous use in America since the eighteenth century, has particular resonance. Classic furniture, including matching Chippendale chairs, a Federal sideboard, and an English dining table set with family silver give the room its personality. I think we struck a happy chord, both in this room and throughout the house, by enriching the decoration to match the evocative setting, but at the same time not overpowering its inherent charm and dignity.

Late-nineteenth-century Persian rugs, used in the living room and dining room, are favored in much of the South. Their red and blue palette constrasts with the yellow and green scheme throughout the house. The painting over the dining room mantel depicts Man o' War, one of the greatest thoroughbred racehorses of all time; it is one of a group of equestrian pictures in the house.

Contemporary Creole

New Orleans, Louisiana

RICK ELLIS AND I OWN AN APARTMENT in the French Quarter of New Orleans—the parlor floor of a modest Creole townhouse built in 1836. The inspiration for its decoration is derived from the early nineteenth century, particularly examples found in and around New Orleans. My goal was to incorporate these historic elements into contemporary decoration.

In the main room, I indulged my fascination with scenic wallpapers found in New Orleans and throughout the South, an interest that I have had since I began my formal study of the decorative arts. I was particularly impressed with the way Henry Francis Du Pont used them at Winterthur (the *Baltimore Alcove* is my favorite) and with the period rooms at the Metropolitan Museum—most notably the Duncan Phyfe sitting room with paper titled *The Monuments of Paris* by Zuber, the nineteenth-century French wallpaper company.

For our small apartment, these formal antique papers would have been inappropriate, a clichéd example of a decorator overdoing his own space. Thus, somewhat chastened and with the memory of a favorite childhood book, *The Story of the Mississippi*, I imagined a new scenic design. Historic examples of scenic papers are typically drawn with the horizon line at one level, so the scene easily continues around the walls of the room. Inspired by the modernist drawings of the book and the custom nature of this paper, which was designed specifically for the room, we were able to "force" the perspective of the horizon so that it dramatically shifts around the room, capturing a variety of scenes along the Mississippi. Beneath the paper and under the chair rail is a base of bright blue—a powerful and fresh color that visually supports the scenes and highlights the colors of the design.

We use this room for dining and for parties, so other than the draped center table, the furniture is pushed to the edges and rearranged as circumstance demands, a tradition from the eighteenth century when formal rooms were similarly organized. Particularly in rooms for parties, having a smaller number of pieces of furniture that can be easily shifted as events demand is better than the fixed furniture plans that are customary today.

FAR LEFT

The exterior trim has been recently repainted with Paris green, a color popular during the first quarter of the nineteenth century. This is considered a Creole townhouse because of the central passageway from the street to the courtyard.

LEFT AND OPPOSITE

In the main room, which we refer to as the mural room, is a neoclassical bookcase with a Louisiana provenance. It holds tableware, vintage cookbooks, examples of natural history, and various souvenirs. The draped table is used for dinner parties and at Mardi Gras for the production of masquerade costumes. The candlesticks are by New Orleans artist Mario Villa.

The neoclassical-style furniture dates to the original period of the house, and is popular in New Orleans. For many designers and clients, this type of furniture is out of favor, but I appreciate how the scale and materials fit the setting. These pieces achieve the balance of both ancient and modern that I often strive for in my rooms.

Another centerpiece of the room is the early Louisiana bookcase that houses part of Rick's collection of books on American cookery, as well as various objects of interest. There is a gilded coconut, a Mardi Gras souvenir from the famous Zulu parade, commemorative cups from the coronation of the last czar of Russia, and a silver tea service from my great-grandparents' house up the Mississippi in Muscatine, Iowa. A cabinet of curiosities is a great device for displaying (and, for that matter, controlling the spread of) meaningful objects of a random nature. I encourage my clients to use these cabinets for the miscellany of life, including trophies, children's art projects, and treasures from travels abroad.

Next door is a sitting room that doubles as a guest room. We painted it pink because, in the end, it was the only color that looked right after the poly-chromy that precedes it and it was popular in nineteenth-century America. The centerpiece is a great daybed that sleeps guests and serves as a sofa for pre-dinner drinks. It once belonged to Jane Englehard, the distinguished collector and patron of the arts. She was a client of Parish-Hadley, and the firm decorated her house for a visit of the Duke and Duchess of Windsor. Albert Hadley, friend and mentor, and I ran into each other at the auction viewing of her estate. When I mentioned that I had come especially to see this bed, he confided, "That it is the bed the Duke used." I am pleased

We refer to the sitting/guest room as the
pink room. It has a mantel typical of New
Orleans Creole architecture. Over the day
bed are late-nineteenth-century German
wood block prints of carnival figures.
Chinese matting, which was commonly
used in American houses for much of the
nineteenth and early twentieth centuries,
covers the floor.

that our guests sleep like royalty in a bed used by one of the most famous houseguests in history. Like its provenance, it is overscaled for the room—this is an example where an oversize piece works, because there are other furnishings to balance the arrangement, particularly the large woodblock prints of German carnival characters. It takes a good eye and willingness to experiment to make unusual plays of scale successful. As this room demonstrates, there are rewards in taking risks in arrangements—and of course, there can be failure to which the best decorators will readily admit.

The bedroom is covered in a reproduction of a French wallpaper that Margaret Pritchard, a curator of prints and maps at Colonial Williamsburg, suggested we use for the restoration of Brooks Bank, the great Virginia plantation, on which I had the opportunity to consult. The pattern, made with twenty-one separate wood blocks, was recreated by the Adelphi Paperhanging Company. Flowered wallpaper is out of fashion right now, but this paper suits the period of our apartment, and I think it has a graphic, contemporary quality. I also like the interesting juxtaposition of this feminine paper against the Audubon print of a California condor. Audubon worked just blocks from our apartment so it is fitting to use one of his prints here. Furthermore, I like its contrasting masculine quality: men who see the room generally admire it and women remark, "Who would want an ugly bird over their bed?" I also see it as an icon of my success working in the South: I always remember that I am a West Coast Yankee finding opportunity in Dixie by attempting good manners and a modicum of taste. Hence I find irony in Audubon's title for his print: "California Vulture."

Balancing Act

Scarsdale, New York

COLLECTORS ARE ALWAYS RETHINKING and recalibrating their homes. This house belongs to one of the foremost collectors of American furniture and decorative arts, along with early Indian and Himalayan sculpture, so there is much to balance here. Furthermore, adding complexity to the design of the house, our clients want to live with their collections in a domestic setting.

Richard Cameron, then working at Ferguson & Shamamian Architects, gently expanded this family home—a 1939 Colonial. The new wings are in the Federal style, suggesting the conceit of later additions to a Colonial house and also allowing the use of neoclassical elements, such as an interior window and three skylights. A top-lit stairwell unites the old and new rooms. Along with period architecture, our decoration of the house referenced traditional decorative elements found in early America, including the use of wallpaper, painted floor cloths, eighteenth- and nineteenth-century upholstery forms, and historic fabrics and carpets. Given the breadth of the American objects, which range from high-style furniture to folk art material, there was no attempt to recreate historically correct period rooms. The clients also amassed Chinese export porcelain and China-trade paintings made specifically for the American market to provide an historic connection between their American and Indian collections, adding another layer of visual and intellectual references to the material culture of late-eighteenth-century America.

The living room features some of the best objects, including a remarkable Chippendale sofa with a distinctive double-peaked camel back, the Logan family piecrust tea table, both from Philadelphia, fine seating furniture from Philadelphia and New York, important case pieces from Salem, Boston, and Philadelphia, and an early John Singleton Copley portrait. The antique furniture is covered with the same types of fabrics that were originally used, including wool damask, horsehair, and leather. Much of the upholstery and the curtains are en suite—as was often the case in the best eighteenth-century American houses—using the same pink wool damask. Care was taken to return the upholstered pieces to their original shapes, which are often lost in re-upholstery. The wallpaper is an early-nineteenth-century pattern, which gives the room visual height. Its complexity also complements the dense arrangement of the furnishings.

The other principal space is an informal sitting room, which is furnished with pieces from the earlier William and Mary period, as well as Queen Anne, Chippendale, and Windsor furniture. This room is papered with a large pattern recreated from an eighteenth-century paper our clients admired in the 1752 Webb House in Wethersfield, Connecticut. I usually rely on using smaller patterns in collectors' houses; however, here the bold pattern works with the strong silhouettes of the furniture and complements a collection of folk paintings and schoolgirl embroidery.

Over the past twenty years, I have come to know the clients' taste and collecting habits well enough to expect regular phone calls soliciting my advice on the purchase of some undeniably beautiful object. I often reply by saying that despite the object's greatness, we will have to work, sometimes very hard, to fit it in. No matter if this object is a large stone sculpture or another Chippendale chair, historic perspective is called up, good decoration prevails, and a happy balance is struck.

The wallpaper in the sitting room is a reproduction of one in the Webb House in Wethersfield, Connecticut. The Windsor furniture suits the room's informal use.

The guest bedroom is furnished with nineteenth-century textiles, including quilts and hooked rugs. The curtains and bed hangings are patterned after the historic models used during the summer. This decoration is reminiscent of rooms at the Winterthur Museum.

ABOVE

The complex decoration of this house is illustrated by this view from the living room through the hall and into the dining room, which shows the three wallpapers used in these rooms.

LEFT

All of the objects in this room— the American pedestal table, the English chairs, and the silver epergne and candlesticks—could have been found in eighteenth- and nineteenth-century houses, save the Indian sculpture in front of the window.

French Taste on Fifth Avenue

New York, New York

THESE GRAND ROOMS ARE LOCATED in the first luxury apartment building on Fifth Avenue and one of the first on the Upper East Side. Designed by McKim, Mead & White in 1910, the building—which was quickly colonized by New York society—galvanized the city's elite to begin moving into apartments. With this groundbreaking structure—one great palazzo—the architects sought to recreate something of the style of the neighboring mansions, many of which had been designed by their firm.

The striking features of this apartment are the Beaux-Arts stone entry hall and reception room, as well as the dining room, the living room, and the study, which is attributed to the famous French decorator Stéphane Boudin. In these interiors, the French boiserie seems entirely of the essence. From the eighteenth century onward, America, like much of the world, looked to France as the epitome of style and luxury. While the French idiom has since lost some of its cachet, until very recently the decoration of almost all the best addresses in the United States were carried out, at least in part, in the French taste.

Indeed, the owners of this apartment are not Francophiles and have contemporary taste. Nevertheless, they chose to build upon its best attributes rather than, as is so often the case, demolish and start over. Furthermore, the light and scale of the rooms are appealing for this large family. They are large, gracious, well laid-out, and can be actively used. We worked to honor the historic nature of the apartment in a fresh way and to make the interiors suitable for a young family.

Originally, the rooms were richly polychromed and gilded—too much so. I am a great believer in the transformative power of color. I counseled that perhaps color—without the gold—would take the edge off the grandeur and make the atmosphere more welcoming. Neutral colors are often used to simplify rooms and make them more modern, but I find this palette is often harsh and ineffective in older rooms. Without the balance of toned paint colors, the scheme can detract from the architecture. After careful planning and consideration, we decided to repaint the walls in shades of blue and green with a strié finish. We strengthened this paint scheme with marbleized bases, and the project was executed deftly and with appropriate restraint by Pierre Finkelstein.

PRECEDING PAGES

The drawing room can successfully seat a substantial number of people. The Indian carpet is early twentieth century.

LEFT AND OPPOSITE

The music room, designed by McKim, Mead & White, incorporates the rich classical detailing that characterizes the firm's work.

We furnished the drawing room with an array of comfortable seating, including upholstered sofas and chairs, benches, and a handsome suite of fauteuils with old white paint labeled by the famous French chairmaker Jacob. These helped strike the right balance in the rooms between the old and new. A smaller sitting room is devoted to music. The color scheme was taken from an original roundel painted with the figure of Euterpe, the muse of music. The decoration of the dining room relies almost completely on a Persian rug colored in shades of aubergine and pistachio. The walls were highlighted in similar shades of green.

The walls are hung with a collection of French and American works on paper, a departure from the old master and Impressionist paintings one might expect in this type of space. The lighter and often more spontaneous nature of the drawings also gives the rooms a more youthful nature.

We set out to create a family-friendly apartment within an important historic context, and our success is proven by how actively it is used. In fact, it is so comfortable that it is renowned among a certain set for old-fashioned birthday parties featuring traditional games like musical chairs and pin-the-tail-on-the-donkey—a rarity on New York's Upper East Side, where children's parties often take on epic proportions outside the home.

A lithograph by Jasper Johns is flanked by other American prints from the twentieth century. The low table is based on one we bought from the collection of the Duke and Duchess of Windsor, which was probably supplied Maison Jansen in the late 1930s. It is possible that Jansen originally decorated this apartment about the same time.

Quiet Colors for Collectors

Wynnewood, Pennsylvania

AT OUR FIRST DESIGN MEETING, our clients mentioned that they wanted to simplify the decoration of this historic house to display their expanding collection of postwar art.

We found the living room walls upholstered in striped silk taffeta, and the curtains lined and interlined with rich valances of swags and jabots. Although well executed, the effect was dated. In contrast, we proposed russet-toned wool for the walls.

To complete the room, we supplied a suite of furniture based on models designed by Jean-Michel Frank in cream silk and plain cream-colored curtains, on simple rods and rings with the only surprising color accent a small yellow cuff. A green and cream brocade on the pillows also provides a modest contrast. The rest of the furniture is from the clients' collection of English and other European antiques.

Our clients resisted even this much color, and we began a lengthy discussion about how their art would look with it. I thought this was an understated choice; they thought it adventurous. After a substantial period of consideration, the russet wall covering was installed, and, in the end, we all agree it makes the art sing.

All the public rooms in the house use brown and green as the basis of their decoration. Our clients came around to our rationale that green performs as neutral color since it can be used alone and combined with any other color. All the rooms also share equally clean upholstery models, antiques, and uncomplicated curtains. At first the clients were hesitant to use any curtains at all, but we counseled that the historic proportions of the rooms, relative to the scale of the windows, demanded this refinement. To minimize the bulk of the panels, they were made with one and a half widths of fabric rather than the usual three. Double pleating, rather than the typical triple pleat, also made a cleaner appearance.

In the breakfast room, the restrained color scheme is furthered by its centerpiece, a Calder mobile, a rare example in all white—even Calder's signature primary colors are not found here. The wicker chairs are stained green to contrast with the wooden cabinets, perhaps in an oblique nod to the dominant color scheme.

ABOVE

The bold graphics of works by Roy Lichtenstein complement the rich architectural detail of the stair hall.

LEFT

Cabinets in the breakfast area evoke the original style of the house. The mobile is by Alexander Calder.

PRECEDING PAGES

Contemporary artworks in the living room include a large portrait by Chuck Close and a sculpture by Lichtenstein.

We deconstructed the existing sun room by removing a cornice made of bullion fringe, a legacy of the 1980s, and refurnished the room with a suite of rattan with modern lines and soft upholstery covered in chartreuse standing against forest-green walls. In this verdant setting, the Roy Lichtenstein in the corner of the room and the Richard Serra on the lawn outside are seen to full advantage.

Upstairs each bedroom is designed around a soft grays. The master bedroom is silver with further hints of yellow.

Of course what our clients meant by "no color" was low-key color, and its use was indeed an effective approach to decorating the house and to displaying the art. When we were photographing the house, the client mentioned that a number of museums now display their postwar art on brown walls—are ideas in the air, or might this be the result of the visits of many museum groups they so generously host?

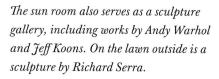

The sun room also serves as a sculpture gallery, including works by Andy Warhol and Jeff Koons. On the lawn outside is a sculpture by Richard Serra.

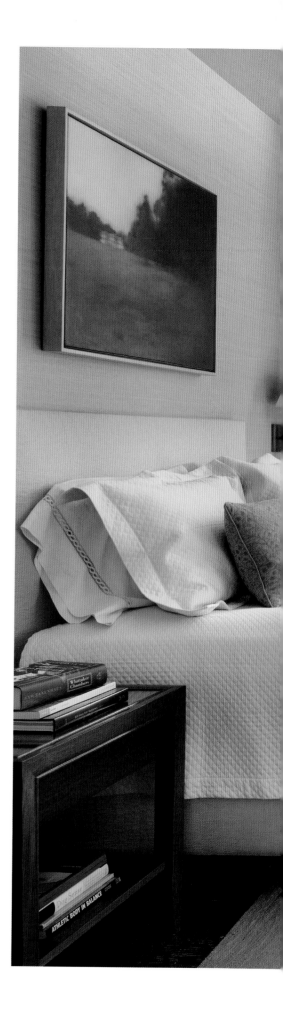

ABOVE

RIGHT

In the guest room, Meter Box, *a sculpture by Donald Judd, is juxtaposed with an English Regency bench.*

Two paintings by Gerhard Richter hang in the master bedroom. The armchairs are nineteenth-century French.

124

Country Life in the Hudson Valley

Dutchess County, New York

WHEN I MET OUR PATRON for this project near Millbrook, New York, she asked us to evoke the spirit of the great Hudson River houses in the design of her new home. Our firm worked together with Peter Pennoyer Architects to create sophisticated architecture and decoration that not only reflected important houses like Montgomery Place by A. J. Davis and the Mills mansion by McKim, Mead & White, but also drew inspiration from their prototypes—the tradition of British country houses shaped by architects and designers such as Robert and James Adam, Henry Holland, and Sir John Soane.

The landscape setting for the house was also carefully considered. Rather than placing the house where it would have long views, it was set low in a valley of small hills—or drumlins—that were formed by glacial deposits. These, in turn, inspired the name of the house—Drumlin Hall. The genius of this location created views up and down the valleys, free of any neighboring buildings; all the rooms have long pastoral outlooks.

All four classical facades of Drumlin Hall were individually designed and relate specifically to the public rooms behind them. In turn, all of the rooms open onto a great central vaulted hall and curved stair. Every space is well proportioned and oriented to take advantage of the views from every side. At the first meeting to discuss the design and decoration, the client made the unusual request to have a formal drawing room in the American neoclassical taste without—notably—the fully upholstered lounge-like furniture that is now universally expected. Immediately, I thought of rooms at Winterthur and those of her fellow collector and friend Richard Jenrette. The ideal would be to make fresh interpretations specific to her.

Typically, Georgian Revival rooms of the early twentieth century, interpreted from eighteenth-century models, were red, blue, or green—like the formal rooms at the White House. At Drumlin Hall, we strove to enliven the interiors by using historic color schemes that are less common. Throughout the house, we used a palette derived from the soft furnishings of the formal drawing room, which included a carpet design dated 6 July 1810 from the archive of Woodward Grosvenor, a British firm in Worcestershire. The principal furnishing fabric is a silk lampas, woven by Prelle in Lyon. The

design is based on a fabric supplied by Duncan Phyfe in 1841. We arranged the furniture, both antique and replica, around an Italian mantel from the 1820s. The curtains and window shades are based on designs published in the nineteenth century. Our client brought with her a growing collection of American paintings, spanning the eighteenth century up to the 1930s. This room displays works by American Impressionists.

In contrast to the formal drawing room, the more relaxed library is furnished entirely with comfortable upholstery. Paintings from the Hudson River School are highlighted.

The second-floor landing has a vaulted ceiling and skylight over the stairwell with niches holding busts by Hiram Powers. We balanced this powerful architecture with a large but informal Indian carpet from Agra and more comfortable chairs; these examples are covered in linen printed with flowers.

One of my favorite rooms is the master bedroom. Here, we incorporated handpainted paper by De Gournay based on nineteenth-century aquatints of the Hudson River that we customized with nearby landmarks like Montgomery Place and Olana, the home of Frederic Church, whose paintings are displayed downstairs. This paper serves as a fitting homage to the great houses of the Hudson Valley and reflects the position of Drumlin Hall among them.

OPPOSITE

All of the first floor rooms open onto the main hall. The principal ornaments in this space are the stair rail by metalworker Jean Wiart wrought in a pattern of garlands, pinecones, and eagles and a life-sized sculpture of Atalanta by William Henry Rinehart.

ABOVE RIGHT

The columns with lion masks and settle were especially designed for the space. The masks represent Atalanta's mythological fate: after a life of forsaking suitors, she took a lover, Melanion, and as a result, an angry god—likely Zeus—turned the couple into lions.

ABOVE LEFT

The gun room is located off of the entrance vestibule. The cabinet as well as the settle and columns in the main hall and the reproduction furniture in the drawing room were made by Harrison Higgins.

PRECEDING PAGES

The drawing room and library were designed to complement each other: the drawing room to receive guests on formal occasions and before dinner and the library for more relaxed occasions and after dinner.

ABOVE AND RIGHT

Sculptures by Hiram Powers and Augustus Saint-Gaudens are grouped with fine Hudson River School paintings in the library.

A generous skylight within a vaulted
ceiling lights the second-floor landing.
All of the four bedrooms in the house
open onto this space, which serves as an
informal sitting room and picture
gallery. We chose the Empire sofa for its
sculptural appearance, softening the
space with the club chairs. A portrait of
the Livingston family adds appreciably
to the atmosphere of the room.

The master bedroom has a bed that, by repute, once belonged to Duncan Phyfe's sister. The scenic wallpaper by De Gournay incorporates views of the Hudson River.

Garden District Glamour

New Orleans, Louisiana

I LIKE TO DECORATE AMERICAN HOUSES in the Greek Revival style, a taste popular in the first half of the nineteenth century. I especially appreciate Southern designs, which often have high ceilings, generous windows, and vigorous classical details. This house, owned by our long-standing friends and clients Julia Reed and John Pearce, is an especially attractive example set in New Orleans's beloved Garden District.

Greek Revival houses can be a challenge for historical purists who rely literally on early-nineteenth-century design sources to redecorate. Earlier and later periods of American design have more direct application to contemporary American taste than the original decoration of houses like these. Their rooms are replete with grandly patterned wallpaper, ornate carpets, heavy curtains (with deep pelmets, multiple fabric panels, and passementerie), and massive "pillar and scroll" mahogany furniture. In sum, this is decoration that is far too much for almost any modern eye to absorb.

For Julia and John's house, there was no appeal for me in creating any archaeological approximation of the original appearance of the house. Conversely, putting together an interior exclusively composed of newly designed furniture would also be a challenge because most contemporary furniture is too small and delicate for the large scale of these rooms. Finally, like most New Orleanians and Southerners, Julia and John generally favor traditional interiors. In essence, to make a contemporary decoration in a Greek Revival house look good, a certain level of invention is required.

With these parameters in mind, I suggested to Julia and John that color would be paramount to the success of their decoration, employing broad expanses of color and an assortment of nineteenth-century furniture that has pleasing proportions but would not have been in New Orleans before the twentieth century. This combination creates successful balance in a room that is somewhat traditional in style, and also youthful and forward-looking. We devised a color scheme that is bold and strong—an old-fashioned combination of green and yellow, based on Julia's memory of her grandmother's house in Nashville, where the renowned decorator Herbert Rogers had used a similar combination of colors. The handsome shade of bright green on the walls in the double parlors is balanced by panels of

ABOVE

Both parlors have black marble mantels that are original to the house. The garniture in the front parlor is a Paris porcelain vase fitted with a clock and a collection of seashells.

RIGHT

The back parlor, where New Orleans's great jazz musicians often play, is loosely furnished with club chairs covered in Le Manach chintz, a rare Colonial armchair, and a piano displaying a sculpture of a golden catfish from a Mardi Gras float.

*The painting of the vulture and a egret
feasting on oysters is by John Alexander.
The rococo-revival chandelier, c. 1870,
could have been used in the original
decoration of this house.*

yellow silk curtains with green fabric flanges. This scheme is complemented
by a vintage chintz we printed from the archive of the Parisian fabric house
Le Manach. A pair of Chinoiserie benches—a purchase we encouraged
before this new house was even found—are covered in a pale green and,
with a grand piano, sit on beige wool mats that are a contemporary
counterpart.

The dining room decoration is centered around a settee from Julia's
grandmother's house. We did not find the color for the walls immediately.
As Albert Hadley counseled, sometimes a room has to be painted several
times before it is right. We worked through several paintdecks and in
the end we found a great color—a blue green that certainly decorates
the room.

The other room on the first floor is the library. Added in the twentieth
century, its relatively modest scale calls for a quieter decor. The walls are
grained to resemble pine. The insides of the bookcases are painted a pale
blue. The curtains are gently patterned in gray, green, and rust. All in all
this retreat is a restful counterpoint to the exuberant decoration in the
neighboring rooms.

Julia Reed's extensive library spans a wide range of American topics from biography to interior design. The African objects are from her travels and the paintings are from John Pearce's family.

Low Country Luxury

Savannah, Georgia

IT WAS A GREAT HONOR when *Town & Country* asked us to decorate a new house at the Ford Plantation near Savannah. In my opinion, show houses need to be believable in order to be a success. Since my work is always shaped by my clients' particular desires, requirements, and the context of a place, I like to conjure a fictional scenario to guide the decoration for show houses. Here, with advice from *Town & Country* editors Pamela Fiori and Sarah Medford, we devised a narrative of a young family: a mother, father, and two children, a boy and a girl. This family was attracted to plantation living with all of its rural activities and charms of the country—especially the waterside where the house is situated. They were, in our mind's eye, traditionalists with a modern bent; for example, they preferred a living room that could be set for dining rather than two separate rooms. They were attracted to artistic things and collected antiques—but not at the price of personal discomfort. This is manifested in a large room at the center of the house, furnished with comfortable seating, a modern dining table after Jean Prouvé, and a great American sideboard.

Architect Jim Strickland, a noted authority on traditional houses in the South, designed this Low Country plantation-style home so that it extended parallel to the water with a large multipurpose room in the center, flanked on one side by a kitchen and a breezeway that connected to a studio and home office. On the other side was a library and another breezeway leading to the master suite and a large screened porch. Two children's rooms and another master bedroom were located upstairs. Our decoration largely played to the water—especially the rooms most closely associated with it. For the breakfast area, we chose a round Saarinen breakfast table with antique lolling chairs around it and, for fun, we added a mobile from the Guggenheim Museum gift shop over it—but not blocking the view. The studio was equally whimsical with an antique sofa, modern sculpture, and kites instead of curtains—again to enhance the view. We took the design of the screened porches more seriously, using practical furniture including Windsor chairs that have an early American history of being used inside and out (Mount Vernon still features them on the front porch). The only slightly novel aspect is the green-painted ceiling, based on a historic example I saw on a porch in North Carolina.

OPPOSITE

The studio is furnished with sculpture on stands, a chair designed by Keith Haring, and a hooked rug. I first saw kites used instead of curtains in the library of an eighteenth-century mansion then owned by a formidable matriarch.

RIGHT

The armchairs around the breakfast table are called lolling chairs— an eighteenth-century term. They are covered in linen case covers— the old-fashioned name for slip covers. The carpet was designed for the room by Elizabeth Eakins.

Two large bedrooms—not including the children's rooms—are somewhat more introspective. We covered the walls of the downstairs room in silk beautifully painted by Lucretia Moroni in a water-like Japanese design. The bed is part of a special group of late-nineteenth-century furniture made of light-colored woods turned to resemble bamboo, a material that has long been used in the tropics and subtropics for making furniture. Plain linen curtains and the sisal matting relax the space.

The upstairs bedroom is dominated by my interpretation of the Southern bed, which often takes advantage of the high-ceilinged rooms typical of the region with elaborate curtains and canopies. Our version is hybridized with beds from the Italian Renaissance in the use of the flat panels of drapery with ribbons and feather bouquets. Joe Biunno, one of New York's best wood and gilding studios, turned the urns, and my partner Rick salvaged the feathers from our Mardi Gras costumes. This bed was the *pièce de résistance* in the house. Our friends in Georgia still refer to the house as the one with the feathers on the bed.

ABOVE

Vesta Heads, *coral sculptures by Oriel Harwood, were controversial when they were first installed, but today, with the popularity of coral in decorative arts, they seem almost understated.*

OPPOSITE

The library is painted to look like cypress, a wood that is often found in historic architecture of this region. A portrait of James Oglethorpe, the founder of Georgia, hangs on the bookshelves. A pillow with an appliqué pattern of a magnolia and the table skirt with special embroidery were made for the house.

OPPOSITE

This large bedroom, with elaborate painted-silk walls, has simple linen curtains. I especially like the sunny effect of yellow curtains, and they appear regularly in my work.

ABOVE

The large upstairs bedroom includes an interpretation of the iconic Southern bed—large, architectural, with elaborate hangings. The portrait is by Alison Nash, an artist who also worked in our office.

A Collector's Garçonnière

New Orleans, Louisiana

MY PARTNER, RICK ELLIS, AND I met Robert Clepper, a New York artist and collector, in New Orleans on a Mardi Gras Day more than twenty years ago. We became the best of friends. And when he announced adverse circumstances were forcing him to leave New York and move to New Orleans, Rick and I offered, as a small consolation, to help him find and decorate his new apartment.

A few weeks later, he sent us to a potential French Quarter address in a Creole townhouse and, after a quick tour—in part because the space is only 350 square feet on two floors—I knew this was the place. But, in order to not inflate the price, as only the endorsement of "a New York decorator" can, I ducked out of the real estate broker's earshot and whispered into my phone, "Buy it, buy it!"

The apartment, the old garçonnière (an extension behind the main house that traditionally housed the elder sons and in-laws) is full of charm, with French doors that open onto a courtyard and gallery and a curved staircase that gives a sense of space that the place does not have. Jessica Harris, who has written widely on the subject, describes Creole as a blending of diverse cultures including European, African, and Native American "with a Caribbean inflection." My challenge, as Robert's friend and decorator, was to exercise restraint and economy, to reinforce the local character of the place, and to pack in as many of his artworks and extensive collections as possible.

When I am decorating, I like to imagine a house from the entrance to the private spaces, particularly the principal bedroom. Although the progression of rooms in this project is brief, it includes the same components of the grandest houses I have worked in—especially if you consider the courtyard as a front hall, the ground floor as old-fashioned living room in the truest sense, and the full-scale stair that benefits the sequence of entering into the master suite. On the ground floor, we included an iron daybed and an old Louisiana worktable that serves for cocktails, dining and, most importantly, for the creation of Robert's collages. Upstairs, an American Empire bed fills the room to the point that the hanging forms a screen for the bath and dressing area.

ABOVE AND OPPOSITE

A rare survival in a garçonnière, the original curved staircase now displays balls of string collected as sculpture. The walls are crowded with small works of art by Damien Hirst, Sally Mann, Cindy Sherman, and Robert Warner.

.

ABOVE RIGHT

The court adjoining the apartment was originally a working yard. Today it functions as an outdoor room, enhanced by old terra-cotta storage jars, iron furniture, and informal subtropical plantings that follow the local traditions.

For the furnishing fabrics upstairs, I selected a glazed chintz based on one in the collection of the Winterthur Museum. The original roller-printed fabric was introduced about 1830—the same decade the house was built. Because of the detail and accuracy of the renderings of the birds, it has also been suggested that the design was influenced by John James Audubon's *Birds of America*. And in addition to the connection of Audubon's New Orleans studio, Robert had a significant collection of bird's nests, so the pattern was more than fitting. This fabric formed the basis of the color scheme.

We fostered the color scheme by maintaining the orange of the late-nineteenth-century screen doors, in part because it is a color especially associated with the Creole architectural tradition in Louisiana, but also because Robert and I both thought there would be challenges and rewards using it. The palette—combining this strong orange with green and pale yellows—is limited because of the small area. We also subtly enriched the space by selecting fabrics with definite textures. Along with the glazed chintz, we used corduroy and taffeta to enrich the decoration, without adding visual distraction in such close proximity.

The real challenge was installing Robert's collections—imagine a puzzle on the grandest scale. As an artist, Robert has a keen eye for arrangement, and Rick, who styles for photography, has an equally acute eye. The two of them spent a week on the inaugural installation. Works by famous artists happily coexist with local prints, drawings, and ephemera and complete this composition in the French Quarter.

The bedroom is furnished with a simple
board table that serves as a desk and
contrasts with the stylish 1840 Empire bed
and gondola chair. The orange plaid
curtains repeat the color of the screen
door. For whimsy, the sheers are embroidered with moth-like creatures.

A Pleasing Play of Pattern

Garrison, New York

WHEN I DECORATED THIS HOUSE in Garrison some fourteen years ago, pattern was popular. It was common to have multiples of them in a single space, and sometimes the most talented decorators, such as Sister Parish and Bunny Williams, would use many as five, six, or even seven in the most beautifully decorated rooms. At that time, the practice of working out full schemes so that there would be continuity and flow within a house and between rooms was not of the paramount importance that it is today.

John Cornforth, one of the foremost scholars of architecture and the decorative arts, pointed out that eighteenth-century English rooms were a patchwork. In turn, America developed its sense of patchwork with its own color schemes and textures that did not necessarily match one another. The genius for successfully mixing patterns is invigorated by an artist's eye—the ability to combine shapes, color, and scale.

Today, the wide use of pattern is largely passé. Most contemporary interiors are monochromatic with no patterns, or they are elephantine in scale. Despite this popular taste, I think this house still looks good because the combinations appear balanced and the architecture is something of a Georgian patchwork itself. One part is eighteenth-century colonial; another section is Greek Revival from the early nineteenth century; and then there is also a Georgian Revival addition from the twentieth century. These additions are easy to detect, and while some of the architectural connections are a bit awkward, the quirks add charm to the house. This is another case in which radical remodeling and removing all of the idiosyncrasies would have lessened the sense of place.

Our first pattern for the scheme was a linen brightly printed with a design of pomegranates and peonies set aside during a project at the client's house in New York. There had not been a place for it there, and I had casually said we would save it for a country house—something that at the time was not even anticipated. We designed roman shades and pillows with the pomegranate fabric. The upholstered furniture is covered in green chenille and two different plaids, a darker version in red, brown, and green for winter and slipcovers of cream and yellow for summer. An old Spanish shawl, embroidered with flowers, is used as a tablecloth.

LEFT

Roman shades in the bay window of the front parlor were ideal since long curtains were impossible to hang here. We used printed linen because of the way the light shines through and juxtaposed its pattern with plaids for the upholstered club chairs and summer slipcovers.

ABOVE

A room devoted to flowers and dogs is papered in a modern flower print designed in 1920s for the Wiener Werkstätte.

As William Morris said, "If there is a reason for keeping the wall very quiet, choose a pattern that works all over without pronounced lines . . . Put very succinctly, architectural effect depends upon a nice balance of horizontal, vertical and oblique. No rules can say how much of each; so nothing can really take the place of feeling and good judgment." We covered the walls of the principal guest room in a chintz with a green trellis design centered with roses. A club chair is upholstered with a celadon strie embroidered with sprigs of leaves. As a bold and unexpected accent, we supplieed an old linen bedcover patterned with ruby red stripes and feathers.In the master bedroom, we used an old-fashioned figural toile with figures rendered in blue and green and a contrasting fringe of pink and yellow on the bed. I hope we achieved the effect that Morris so clearly describes.

Adding to the charm of the place is a small one-room outbuilding set on the hill behind the main house overlooking the Hudson Valley. Known as the Wendy House after Wendy's diminutive playhouse in *Peter Pan*, it was built as a folly and retreat with antique paneling from an eighteenth-century house in Bedford, Massachusetts. We added a pair of Morris chairs, actually made by his firm rather than the imitations that also bear his name, and covered them with English blocked linen.

The porch at the back of the house, the principal outdoor space, has no pattern—perhaps a portent of the largely patternless decoration today. Still the interiors of this house serve as a reminder of the beauties of combining patterns and creating pleasing visual complexity in interior design.

The Federal bed has a wooden canopy draped in gauze and trimmed with block fringe. The full-length curtains—somewhat overstated for a country bedroom—soften the architecture of the room, which has many doors and windows.

LEFT

The main room in the Wendy house (as in Peter Pan) has a bright green floor and a pair of chairs by William Morris. The fireplace wall from an eighteenth-century house in Bedford, Massachusetts, was installed when the house was built in the early twentieth century.

BELOW

The dining room features a large collection of antique brass candlesticks, displayed here on an eighteenth-century patterned tablecloth.

OPPOSITE

The porch is furnished with an old country table, Windsor chairs, and benches made by the caretaker.

Fire Island Idyll

Point o' Woods, New York

THE IDYLLIC HOUSE AT THE BEACH— small and straightforward— has a particular hold on our memory. There is something about the scale and simplicity that conjures the perfect and carefree summer day. This beach cottage, built in 1895, captures the essence of this ideal. It has just four small bedrooms, a sitting room, a dining area, a galley kitchen and, what really makes the house work, the quintessential summer porch— the place where most of action occurs.

The colorful decoration was inspired in part by a bright red wicker chair that had come with the house, along with the bright blue frames for the screens. (I surmised from the vast amount of red, white, and blue and the myriad patriotic emblems we found in the house that the last time it was decorated was for the bicentennial celebration of 1976.) Incorporating furnishings the clients already own and sometimes pieces left by previous owners can direct the interior design in ways that one might not immediately imagine, but here they offer a sense of visual continuity and history that starting afresh might not have. This type of recycling must be voluntary, since forcing the reuse of furniture is the nemesis of good decoration. In this case, these inherited objects add substantially to the relaxed feel of the place and recall generations of summer pleasure.

When the owners purchased the house, the wood walls of the shadowy sitting room were a point of discussion. Many informal advisers proposed that the walls be painted white to "freshen and lighten the place up." I countered that the walls were an original feature that give this cottage a particular character. Advocates of white walls claim that they "allow the view to come in," and make the rooms seem bigger. In my experience, white rooms often have little mystery, and it is patently clear where the corners are and just how much space there really is. With their edges in shadow, darker rooms can have a sense of expanse. Here, the view of the trees is important, and the medium brown of the paneling frames it in a neutral way rather than distracting from it.

Beach houses call for simple but not necessarily lesser-quality furniture. This room is centered with two chairs of particular note by the great Arts and Crafts master Gustav Stickley. The flat-weave Guatemalan carpet, made for us by Stark, provides an informal texture and palette.

This design of the attic bedroom is another example of incorporating a contribution from the owner. In this case the clients' daughter selected a tie-dyed bed cover as an independent expression of her identity. Its strong design is balanced by the intimate nature of the ceiling with its dormers and the simplicity of the other furnishings.

Although the ocean is just yards way, the house has no direct view except from a "lifeguard" chair on the second-floor deck. This also came with the house, and it is another demonstration of the nostalgic and contemporary use of this classic cottage.

ABOVE

The exterior of the house, apart from new shingles, has remained much the same for more than one hundred years. The "lifeguard" chair has a panoramic view of the ocean and the bay that surround Fire Island.

OPPOSITE

A built-in bench, an original feature of the house, is large enough to double as a daybed. For most of the upholstery, we used waterproof canvas as a defense against wet swimsuits.

ABOVE

The blue-painted floor contrasts with the wicker dressing table and the pink drop-leaf table, which came with the house. We added the yellow lamps and the pique assiette *mirror.*

RIGHT

Furnishings in the daughter's room include her tie-dyed bedcover, a chest of drawers by George Nelson, and a small wire table by Charles and Ray Eames.

ABOVE

In the dining room, a painted picnic table is surrounded by a set of English Arts and Crafts chairs. The painting of beach balls is by Donald Baechler.

LEFT

Along with the red wicker chair and the blue screen frames, the porch is furnished with modern dining furniture and a large daybed designed especially for the children and their friends.

An Old-Fashioned Porch Down East

Mount Desert, Maine

BECAUSE OUR CLIENT HAD SPENT her entire life in historic houses—two in South Carolina and another in London—we were surprised when she showed us her entirely new house in Maine. She bought it because of its spectacular site and, she admitted almost hesitantly, because everything worked. There were no sticking windows, leaking roofs, or other "old house issues" that she had spent vast energies coping with over the years. Ironically, we immediately set out to take the new edge off the place and instill many of the vintage charms she missed. The addition of a generous porch was key to this endeavor. In Maine's summer season, which seems like a millisecond, it is no wonder that those who summer there try to extend this brief window by building porches with fireplaces.

Unlike the typical front porches of many older American houses, this porch qualifies as a full-fledged room. Anchored by a very large fireplace, it reflects an American vernacular associated with the wilds of the Adirondacks and the Far West. Designed by Keith Kroeger, the porch sits at the end of the house. The indoor living room opens to the porch's large sitting area, which we furnished traditionally with an old Persian carpet, antique wicker painted an old-fashioned green, and a simple low table. With the plain furniture forms, we tried not to compete with the fireplace. Off to the side, near a door to a library, we added a dining table and chairs, a buffet, and—one of my favorite devices—an outdoor mirror that reflects the quickly changing summer sky.

In the living room, we arranged comfortable seating around the central fireplace. For the upholstery, we were drawn to a classic Lee Jofa linen print with a very large-scale pattern, both for its impact and color. It would have been too powerful to cover entire pieces, so we opted to upholster the outside with plain linen to frame and accentuate the pattern.

The stair hall is lined with prints from the famous portfolio *Twenty Birds of Mount Desert* by the Philadelphia artist and ornithologist Carroll Tyson. They were relatively simply framed, and we arranged them to imply paneling—an approach that strengthens the space. Collections of personal objects perfectly arranged set the tenor for the whole house.

ABOVE

To "tone" the house into the neighborhood of older homes, we advised that all the woodwork be painted a dark green popular in coastal Maine. The addition of the large porch set into a rocky outcropping also helped the house appear more settled in its landscape.

RIGHT

The massive stone fireplace is used throughout the foggy Maine summers.

The dining room has a classic Georgian pedestal table, the most functional of models, easily opened and closed, and stable on its tripod bases. The chairs, perhaps a bit fancy for Maine, are family pieces.

RIGHT ABOVE

The house is sited on the inland edge of a fiord.

RIGHT BELOW

The stair hall has a British Colonial center table and a French lantern we found in London. The stacks of books and the arrangement of objects give the house an immediate sense of welcome.

The living room is centered around a
splendid low table made of burled maple
and matched leather panels. A collection
of English chairs provides seating for
frequent house parties. The settee and
two chairs in the living room have backs
and seats of tea-stained flowered linen
that we combined with solid green backs
and sides to "contain" the large pattern.

East Brick

Nantucket, Massachusetts

NANTUCKET, ONCE AN IMPORTANT and bustling whaling village, is rich in architecture and charm. This house—known locally as one of the "three bricks"—reflects this tradition. Built in 1838 as a wedding present for a son of Joseph Starbuck, one of the island's most successful businessmen, this Federal house is notable for its distinguished proportions and scale. Later it was owned by two old-line American families; Jane Engelhard, the great patron of American arts and letters, also used the house for more than thirty years.

I am a firm believer that it is often better to adapt to a house rather than to force the architecture to adapt to you. In approaching this project, I offered my usual advice, recommending that my clients live in the house before remodeling it.

Some had suggested that the place be updated by removing the back of the house—a series of beautifully detailed bedrooms and porches—and replacing it with an "up-to-date" master bedroom suite. With the support of architects Botticelli and Pohl, I countered this ill-conceived idea. Since the old spaces were so handsome, and the house was to be a summer home, I proposed that we simply remodel the existing master bath and add two showers to the guest rooms. This way we were able to maintain appreciably more of the historic fabric of the house. At the same time, we preserved all the existing antique hardware, even if it did not all match, repaired the old floors—but did not sand them—and repainted the original woodwork without removing all signs of use and age. Now the house is in good antiquarian condition, but does not look new.

As decorator, I had the challenge of incorporating the beautiful Federal architecture and the collection of American paintings and antiques into a fresh, viable family home. The classic double parlors at the front of the house divided by a central hall were, by nature of the plan, formal. Historically, the front parlors were used for entertaining and the spaces away from the street for dining and a library. However, to temper their formality, we made sure to employ the classic American model of comfort— the sort that Sister Parish and Albert Hadley preached as gospel. We always made sure there was ample upholstered seating in every room, light to read by, and places to put drinks and refreshments. By incorporating our clients' collections as well as objects that appealed to them, we were able to personalize the space and make the rooms more livable.

Throughout, curtains based on styles associated with early-nineteenth-century architecture flatter the historic proportions of the interiors. The swags also reflect the long tradition of this style of curtain in American decoration—a form that has become archaic only in the last twenty years with the universal advent of rings and poles, if curtains are used at all. And, in the dining room, some early-twentieth-century built-ins were preserved for their history and quirky charm. In one bay is a display of historic artifacts and materials uncovered during the renovation.

Since seafaring and trade with Asia were so important to New England and Nantucket, we incorporated many examples of Chinese Export wares, including ceramics, lacquerware, and paintings. We combined these with American paintings with Nantucket associations and English and American decorative arts from the eighteenth and early nineteenth centuries to create what can be considered historically as an American interior—one that reflects its surroundings and draws on European sources as only an eclectic American room can.

Our clients had a penchant for Chinese wallpaper—paper that was first imported to America thorough the China trade in the late eighteenth and early nineteenth centuries. While there was no evidence that it was used in Nantucket in a substantial way, we still liked its historic appeal and used it in the stair hall and the master bedroom. We found that its organic pattern relaxed the formal spaces and looked especially appealing in the summer light.

However, it is the attic that really makes the house work for the owners. Beneath the eaves, there was a series of small bedrooms, originally designed as maids' quarters. These have been furnished traditionally with antique iron beds, with an eye to the daughters of the house. Here, a central space with a television and comfortable seating provides a retreat. Above this space is a four-sided glazed cupola with panoramic views of the island. On one side of the cupola is a small door—the size of a pane of glass—which by repute Mrs. Engelhard's butler would use to furtively smoke. Not that we encourage smoking, but we saved this historic element as another nod to the long history of this house.

ABOVE

The breakfast room, which overlooks the garden, is used for family meals.

OPPOSITE

The blue of the wallpaper is a favorite color of our clients. By using it in the stair hall, we were able to thread it throughout the house. The newel post's original ivory button was one of the many period details we maintained in the house.

On the ground floor there are four rooms or parlors, two on each side of the central hall. The front rooms are formally decorated in related schemes for entertaining. Each has a glass chandelier and English chairs that simulate bamboo. The back parlors serve as a library and dining room. The caned panels were installed in the 1920s to conceal the radiators.

The turned bedstead in the guest room was made in New England; an early map of Nantucket hangs above it. In the master bedroom, we retained the Colonial Revival bookcase beside an original mantel supported on Ionic columns.

LEFT

Inside the cupola is the window with a small door that Mrs. Engelhard's butler installed to accommodate his smoking.

BELOW

We kept the remarkable truss work of the attic exposed and gave it a summery coat of white paint.

OPPOSITE

The attic bedrooms, now used by the daughters of the house, are furnished with iron beds. Mrs. Parish once counseled that only maids had metal beds, but they are, of course, now appreciated for their stylish sculptural shapes.

Western Splendor

New Mexico

SET ON 120,000 ACRES IN THE ARID LANDS of northeastern New Mexico, Diamond A Ranch is anchored by a nineteenth-century adobe building—once a stagecoach stop on the route from Lincoln to Roswell—that was expanded into a house in the twentieth century. Herbert Bayer, an abstract artist and modernist architect, designed the ranch's Territorial-style main building in 1964, based on the plain geometries of historic New Mexican buildings for a former owner, oilman and art collector Robert O. Anderson. At the same time, a seventeenth-century Irish-oak-paneled library, removed from the Huntington mansion in Hillsborough, California, was added to the house, furthering the architectural complexity of the compound. I well remember the first time our client described the ranch to me, especially this room, replete with silver chandeliers. Recently Peter Pennoyer has added a commodious dining room, a leather-paneled bar, guest rooms, and handsome courtyards.

As decorator, my goal was to artistically relate this diverse collection of rooms, reflecting the region's heritage without falling into clichés of Southwest decoration. Historically, houses in New Mexico were furnished with a combination of locally made furniture, often in the Hispanic tradition, decorative arts from Europe and Asia and, after the establishment of railroads from the eastern United States, furniture manufactured there. The furnishings for this ranch followed in this vein.

The nineteenth-century rooms of the adobe wing were dilapidated. As part of the project, with the careful restoration of the *latillas*, these spaces were turned into rustic guest rooms. The adobe preservation work was done by Edward and Jess Crocker, whose firm is dedicated to traditional adobe technique. Our decoration complemented the textured adobe walls, waxed clay and dirt floors, and ceilings with an appropriate variety of antiques, including a French daybed, an Empire mirror, and a side chair made in New Mexico. These spartan guest rooms were balanced by luxurious bedrooms upstairs, created out of nondescript spaces that had been used to display Anderson's modern art collection.

The adobe wing opens onto the Spanish Room. The center of the house, this room serves as both a luxurious oasis amid the arid ranch lands as well as anchor to the organization of the adjoining rooms. The walls are also adobe here, with old-fashioned printed chintz curtains and silk velvet sofas for contrast. All the metalwork, including the tables, curtain hardware, and sconces was designed for the room and made by Paul Ferrante in California.

Adjoining the Spanish Room via a leather-paneled bar is the library with its great paneled walls of Irish oak. We restored the woodwork and added the plaster friezes and ceiling, giving the room more classical proportions and details. As a foil, the new dining room was designed with an arched and coffered ceiling covered in gold stars.

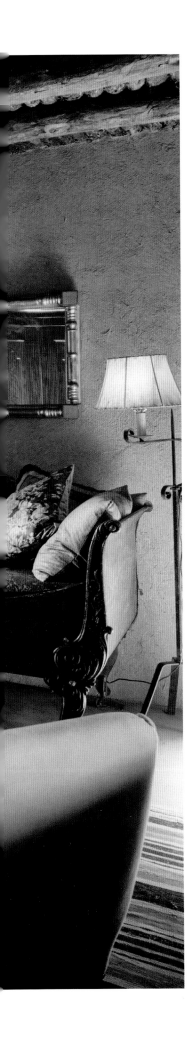

In the adobe wing, the vigas *(beams)*
and latillas *(laths) in the ceiling and*
the compacted dirt floor were restored
to their nineteenth-century appearance.
In the newer part of the house, the
bedrooms are less rustic.

East End Views

Southampton, New York

THIS HOUSE IN THE SEASIDE resort of Southampton, New York, has an ideal location between the ocean and the bay. It is most definitely at the beach, but it is also part of a community where people still get dressed up for cocktails and dinner and thus require handsome rooms for entertaining. So, central to this house is a grand drawing room that is a balance between a traditional drawing room and the less formal living rooms more popular today.

As in many of my rooms, an old carpet is the focal point of the design. Here, it is a worn nineteenth-century English Axminster rug with an antique-red ground, once the foundation of an enriched room, perhaps on the scale of a great British neoclassical country house by Robert Adam. Now relaxed by age and wear, it serves to balance Peter Pennoyer's classic but streamlined architecture.

The tall French doors opening out to the views of the ocean and the subtle pink and green color scheme—most notably seen in the green-trimmed curtains and their pink-painted rings and the matching painted pink mirror frame—reinforce the resort nature of the room. Pink and green is not a color scheme I select without pause, as it can sink a room into saccharine cliché quickly. However, with its long tradition in storied resort towns like Southampton and Palm Beach, I think it offers a fresh recollection of a classic and beloved color combination.

The furniture in the room is largely classical, with new armless chairs and the linen-wrapped low tables to update a furniture plan that accommodates large groups in convivial arrangements. The buoyant nature of Matisse's famous Jazz series also serves as a modern foil.

Just beyond the drawing room is a more casual sitting room that opens onto the porch and pool. A simple seagrass carpet with a leather border gives the space a beach-like quality. To provide a visual balance between the two rooms, the curtains have been richly appliquéd and embroidered with a Georgian pattern contemporaneous with the antique carpet.

LEFT

Penn and Fletcher—who also embroider for haute couture—executed the curtain borders, a pattern that was inspired by an eighteenth-century book of designs. The use of pink within the pink-and-green scheme is subtle—just the curtain rings, some of the trims, and the mirror frame in the living room.

RIGHT

The French doors open to the pool, beach, and ocean immediately outside.

The octagonal dining room is located on the other side of the drawing room. Polygonal plans almost always result in interesting decoration. Here, the scale of the space is enhanced by a pair of large antique mirrors on the end walls. The chandelier is fitted with hurricane shades and real candles. In an oblique acknowledgment of the house's nautical location, we incorporated a boat winch to easily raise and lower the fixture.

Capping these rooms is a tower room. Rising above the ridges of the roof, it offers long vistas of the ocean, beach, and bay from all sides—a rare space with 360-degree views. Since the windows are the defining feature, I chose to focus on them, framing the views with stenciled window shades.

LEFT

The upholstered dining room chairs were known as back stools when the style was created in the eighteenth century. They are examples of early modern comfort.

ABOVE

The eighteenth-century low table in the library is a period example of a style still popular today.

LEFT

The tower room, with windows on four sides, feels like a porch. It has an Arts and Crafts table and British colonial chairs.

RIGHT

We painted the front hall entirely in a bright green to introduce the sequence of public rooms on the first floor. The English Chippendale table displays a giant ceramic shell filled with sand and shells from the beach.

BELOW

A view of the house across the wetlands that border the house. The tower is part of the recent addition.

Penobscot Perch

North Haven, Maine

HOUSES IN COASTAL MAINE are forced by nature to have practical exteriors with simple details in low relief to deflect the harsh climate. In contrast, their interiors often feature handsome volumes and refined elements, such as classical mantels, cornices, and paneled walls. Many rooms have nautical qualities—derived from the region's maritime tradition—and stunning water views.

We decorated this house for a sailing family that embraces these traditions. Peter Pennoyer designed the house using a restrained version of the shingle style that the summer people had favored for building houses on the island since the turn of the twentieth century. The plan follows the geography of the curving bluff. Rooms angle out toward the view and seem almost to sail on the water.

The dining room at the center of this plan is perhaps the most nautical, and recalls the wheelhouse of a boat. It is painted ivory to frame rather than contrast with the view. At night, when views are lost to the darkness, the room still looks good because a set of neoclassical chairs, painted in shades of blue and green, take visual precedence. Complementing them is a set of sconces with glass shades etched with woodland scenes and Native Americans posed with bows and arrows. We covered the chairs in a pattern of eucalyptus leaves—in part as a bow to nature in general, but also to our clients' time in California.

The living room has remarkable views on two sides that almost overwhelm the room with their visual power. We furnished it with large, old-fashioned sofas covered in red wool—which is atypical of my work. When our client casually asked for this color, I was surprised because I usually try to downplay large upholstered pieces with more neutral colors. I conjured in my mind historic examples of red sofas, including several from my own childhood, and we began to incorporate them into the plan. For me, this affirmed that a dialogue with clients leads to richer and more personal interiors. Elizabeth Eakins made the carpet based on an early hooked rug. The scale of the design and its artisanal qualities have the vigor to balance the view.

ABOVE

The exterior features the gables and irregular massing of the shingle style.

RIGHT

The low table and the leather trunk are both Chinese. The Maine islands, often enveloped in fog, remind me of Chinese paintings so I especially like to use Asian pieces here.

OPPOSITE

In the living room, the fireplace surround is Moroccan tiles, which look especially good in new shingle style houses. Their complex shapes, small scale, artisanal surface, and handsome colors relate closely to the art tiles used in the original late-nineteenth-century houses.

The library is the only inward-facing public room. We made it purposefully introspective. Panels of red linen curtains—the only dramatic curtains in the house—set in arched reveals screen the view and, perhaps as a subconscious nod to the ocean beyond, we painted the whole room in a bright, old-fashioned eighteenth-century turquoise. The inclusion of the piano and family furniture furthered the personal and historic connections.

The progression through the house culminates in the master suite. In the bedroom, we adapted historic paneling from the early shingle style houses in Newport. Because of economics and new situations, I find it best to make spirited interpretations rather than literal copies in new houses. In the master bath, simply configured around yet another expansive view, we incorporated a whimsical interior touch. During a design meeting, I tentatively asked to paper the ceiling with a pattern of leaves and birds—an impractical proposal, of course, because wallpapers often peel in steamy bathrooms. Our clients, who are practical people, also understood the beauty of an interior flourish and, acknowledging the tradition of Maine vernacular, said yes.

PRECEDING PAGES

The new carpet in the library was made by Darius based on an Indo Tabriz design. The paneling with curtain pockets follows examples by Delano & Aldrich that Peter Pennoyer and I admired.

LEFT

Especially in larger houses, I like to ensure each room has its own character. Often we achieve this with distinctive paint colors as we did in the coatroom, where I promised our client that no one else had one with iron red walls and a bright blue floor.

OPPOSITE

The breakfast room has chairs copied from eighteenth-century New England originals. The windows are fitted with glass shelves to display collections of colored glass—a device popular with early collectors of Americana.

LEFT

The alcove of the master bedroom is furnished in a nineteenth-century fashion with two antique upholstered chairs, a ship model, and a portrait by Paul César Helleu.

ABOVE

The master bath also has an alcove, this one furnished with a bathtub placed with a commanding view.

Project Credits

House with the Golden Stair
New York, New York
2002
Senior Designer: Ali Schwarz
Architect: Basil Walter

Youthful Historicism
New York, New York
1996
Senior Designers: Erik Smith,
Katherine Snead
Architect: Peter Pennoyer and
Gregory Gilmartin of Peter Pennoyer
Architects

High Style Americana
New York, New York
2009
Senior Designer: Egan Seward
Architect: Boris Baranovich
Architects, PC

A Place of their Own
New York, New York
2011
Senior Designer: Egan Seward
Architect: Josh Brandfonbrener

A Designer's Legacy
New York, New York
1998 to present
Senior Designers: Egan Seward,
Erik Smith

Decoration as Collage
Philadelphia, Pennsylvania
2002
Senior Designer: Ali Schwarz

Enriched Decoration
New York, New York
2012
Senior Designer: Marissa Stokes

Pied à Terre for the Past
Charleston, South Carolina
1998
Senior Designer: Erik Smith
Architect: John Laurens

Ancient Allée
Green Pond, South Carolina
2005
Senior Designer: Betsy Greenway
Carney
Architect: Schmitt Walker Architects,
Charleston, South Carolina

Contemporary Creole
New Orleans, Louisiana
2006
Architect: Frank A. Masson

Balancing Act
Scarsdale, New York
1998 to present
Senior Designer: Erik Smith
Architect: Richard Cameron of
Ferguson & Shamamian Architects

French Taste on Fifth Avenue
New York, New York
1998
Senior Designer: Erik Smith

Quiet Collectors
Wynnewood, Pennsylvania
2001–2009
Senior Designers: Christa Kelly,
Marissa Stokes

**Country Life in the
Hudson Valley**
Dutchess County, New York
2009
Senior Designer: Egan Seward
Architect: Peter Pennoyer, Thomas P.
R. Nugent, and Gregory Gilmartin of
Peter Pennoyer Architects

Garden District Glamour
New Orleans, Louisiana
2006
Senior Designer: Egan Seward
Project Manager: Marissa Stokes
Architect: Lewis Graeber

Low Country Luxury
Savannah, Georgia
1999
Senior Designer: Erik Smith
Architect: Jim Strickland of Historical
Concepts

A Collector's Garçonnière

New Orleans, Louisiana

2003

A Pleasing Play of Pattern

Garrison, New York

1997

Project Managers: Erik Smith,
Katherine Snead

Consulting Architect, Porch Addition:
Stephen Killcoyne

Fire Island Idyll

Point o'Woods, New York

2002

Senior Designer: Erik Smith

Architect: Peter Pennoyer and James
Taylor of Peter Pennoyer Architects

An Old Fashioned Porch
Down East

Mount Desert, Maine

2009

Senior Designers: Egan Seward,
Erik Smith

Architect: Keith Kroeger of Keith
Kroeger Associates

East Brick

Nantucket, Massachusetts

2008

Senior Designer: Egan Seward

Architect: Botticelli & Pohl Architects

Western Splendor

Lincoln County, New Mexico

1999

Senior Designers: Erik Smith, Will
Hooper

Architect: Peter Pennoyer, Gregory
Gilmartin, and Anik Pearson of
Peter Pennoyer Architects

East End Views

Southampton, New York

1997

Senior Designer: Erik Smith

Architect: Peter Pennoyer, Gregory
Gilmartin, and Kevin Dakan of
Peter Pennoyer Architects

Penobscot Perch

North Haven, Maine

2005

Senior Designers: Lori Greene,
Jennifer Bernstein

Architect: Peter Pennoyer, Gregory
Gilmartin, and James Taylor of
Peter Pennoyer Architects

Peter Aaron: 194–98, 200, 201 top

Andrew Bordwin: 16, 17, 19 top

Scott Frances: 22–29

Reto Halm: 204–5, 206, 210 left,
211 bottom

Maura McEvoy: 146–153

Keri McCaffety: 90–94, 96–97,
154–59, 176–83, 186, 188–91,
192 top, 193

Jeff McNamara: 78–83

Pieter Estersohn: 30–39, 40–49,
50–57, 58–67, 68–77, 84–89, 98–107,
108–15, 116–25, 126–37, 138–45,
160–67

Robert Reck: 199, 201 bottom

William Waldron: 14, 15, 18,
19 bottom, 20, 21, 94–95, 202–3,
207–9, 211 top

Jonathan Wallen: 168–75, 184, 185,
187, 192 bottom, 212–21